THE CHAMBER PLAYS

First published in 1991 by Absolute Classics, an imprint of
Absolute Press, 14 Widcombe Crescent, Bath, England

© Eivor Martinus 1991

Cover and text design: Ian Middleton

Photoset and printed by The Longdunn Press Ltd, Bristol
Bound by W.H. Ware & Son, Clevedon
Cover printed by Devenish and Co., Bath

ISBN 0 948230 41 X

THE CHAMBER PLAYS

August Strindberg

Translated by Eivor Martinus

a b s o l u t e   c l a s s i c s

INTRODUCTION

In 1888 Strindberg proudly announced the birth of the Naturalist drama with MISS JULIE. *"Ceci datera,"* (this will go down in history) he told his publisher prophetically, but it did not have the desired effect. The play was rejected and remained unplayed for eighteen years in his native Sweden. Undaunted, he went on to write nine one-act plays with a strong central theme, a simple set and a probing psychological argument.

At the time, he was hoping to start an experimental theatre in Copenhagen but the first production of MISS JULIE there was a total fiasco; the Scandinavians were not ready for their innovative writer yet.

At the *Freie Bühne*, Berlin, Strindberg enjoyed successes with THE FATHER, MISS JULIE and CREDITORS in the early nineties and at Antoine's *Théâtre Libre* in Paris a production of MISS JULIE even beat Ibsen's record in 1893. Spurred by this success he thought of starting his own theatres in those cities.

During his brief marriage to the Austrian journalist Frida Uhl in the nineties, there were even plans to start a Strindberg theatre in London and his wife stayed behind in England after their honeymoon there to discuss the project with Heinemann and J.T. Grein. But none of these plans came to fruition. It was August Falck, the young theatre director who introduced MISS JULIE in Sweden in 1906, who was to become Strindberg's partner and co-producer. They worked together for five tempestuous years and created the first real 'fringe' theatre in Sweden. The Intimate Theatre opened in November 1907 and closed three years later because of financial difficulties. Considering the relative short life-span and the shoe-string productions that were staged there, it is the more remarkable that the theatre has made such a lasting impression.

When asked to explain what he wanted to achieve with his new type of theatre Strindberg said:
"If you ask me what does an Intimate theatre want, and what is meant by Chamber plays, I'll answer like this: In drama we're looking for the meaningful theme but with certain limitations. In the treatment of it we avoid all ostentation and all calculated effects. – The author should not be tied by any specific form because the theme

determines the form – so freedom in execution, only restricted by the unity of concept and the feeling of style."

The general mood in the Chamber plays is sombre. They are dramas about souls waking up from an infernal dream, preparing for their last combat with the world before retiring – sleepwalkers who learn to see without a film over their eyes. All the main characters discover the truth about themselves or their origin in a moment of revelation. In order to emphasize the more spiritual aspect of these late plays Strindberg pressed for a diffuse set in the style of a Turner painting. Ideally, he wanted a back-cloth that could easily be replaced and the stage props should be few but exquisite; they were often in fact supplied by himself.

As an homage to Beethoven he decided to number the plays like musical compositions, hence THUNDER IN THE AIR (OVÄDER is Opus 1, AFTER THE FIRE (BRÄNDA TOMTEN) Opus 2, THE GHOST SONATA (SPÖKSONATEN) Opus 3, and THE PELICAN (PELIKANEN) Opus 4. The little known last chamber play, THE BLACK GLOVE (SVARTA HANDSKEN) which is rarely mentioned in discussions about the chamber plays, was obviously intended as a supplement because Strindberg called it Opus 5. It is obviously no coincidence that Strindberg borrowed musical terms to create a new type of drama.

Miss Lind-af-Hageby mused in 1927: "It is strange how often one is constrained to use musical metaphors in describing Strindberg's style. There is always music in his language. He was conscious of this himself for in his last plays he always chose music to fit the mood of his dramatic movement."

Strindberg was a keen and able amateur musician who was rarely without an instrument. Even during his long travels abroad he brought his guitar with him. The last few years of his life were greatly enhanced by his regular musical evenings in his own home where he became friends with two talented young composers, Stenhammar and Aulin. "Music deafens the pain," he said.

Structurally and thematically, the five plays have a lot in common. The main 'character' in all these five plays is an apartment block in the centre of Stockholm, this "tower of Babel" that is described so graphically in THE BLACK GLOVE:
"A tower of Babel with all kinds of people

and languages; six flights of stairs and a basement
three apartments on each floor
a dozen cradles and seven pianos.

here a newly-wed and there a divorcee
and over there a widower.
Jumbled up like their pianinos
between them producing a waltz
a fugue and a sonata."

A kind of middle-class Swedish Coronation Street in other words. It
is easy to imagine all the action taking place in the same apartment
block; the various plays concentrating on one family at a time,
culminating in a baroque mixture of realism and fantasy. The stories
interweave and cross each other's paths until in the end a clear pattern
emerges.

Old men turn up in all the plays, except THE PELICAN, where the
father-figure features prominently *in absentia* instead. The Man in
Opus 1, THUNDER IN THE AIR, says he is looking forward to the
peaceful existence of old age, but his restless behaviour, his nervous
interest in Gerda, the young beautiful ex-wife belies a passionate
nature that refuses to be quenched quite yet. It is an ironic story
about a man who is trying to adapt to a bourgeois *modus vivendi* but
who is inevitably drawn to the chaos of a more Bohemian life-style,
here represented by Gerda and her mysterious husband whose hands
move like those of a gambler: "Shuffle and deal, shuffle and deal."

In Opus 2, AFTER THE FIRE, there are old men scattered
throughout the play. They are there as reminders of the past and they
make up the backbone of the community: the bricklayer, the stone
mason, the hearse driver and the landlady of the public house, The
Last Nail. Like in THUNDER IN THE AIR the two main
characters are brothers but in this play all that is left of the
respectable childhood home is the ruins of a burnt-down house. "In
old age, when your eye sees, you realise that those funny figures make
up a pattern, a code, an ornament, a hieroglyph which can only be
interpreted when it is finished: this is life. The world weaver has
woven it."

Opus 3, THE GHOST SONATA takes us a step further away from
realism and into a nightmare setting. Not only is the past revealed to
be a sham, but the characters carry on a ghost-like existence and

redemption is only possible through the sacrifice of the young innocent couple. It is a deeply pessimistic play but at the same time it has a bleak sense of humour.

Opus 5, THE BLACK GLOVE has two old men at the centre again, echoing THUNDER IN THE AIR. Here they represent wisdom and folly in the guise of the learned gentleman in the garret and common sense in the caretaker who leads a mole-like existence in the basement.

Young love, children, flowers and music are always the redeeming features in these plays. For instance, Louise, the young relative in THUNDER IN THE AIR who is described by The Man as "a beautiful young girl whose very presence fills me with joy, like when you look at a work of art without necessarily wanting to own it." In AFTER THE FIRE there is the blue-eyed young couple about to be married; in THE GHOST SONATA the Student and the Hyacinth girl declare their eternal love while all the other human relationships around them are proved false; in THE PELICAN there is the brother and sister, the innocent sufferers, caught between the scheming mother and her son-in-law; in THE BLACK GLOVE Strindberg introduces the young servant girl, wrongly accused of stealing; all these characters help to relieve the gloom, despair and cynicism found in the chamber plays. They represent goodness in the shadow of evil.

Another recurring theme is the child used as a weapon to punish one of the characters. In THUNDER IN THE AIR a child is being abducted and there are hints at possible child abuse even; in THE BLACK GLOVE another young child is returned to her mother at the end of the play and both these two mothers happen to be called Gerda. The suffering young bride in THE PELICAN is also a Gerda. The child is the highest good, the child is the greatest gift in life, according to Strindberg. August Falck, who was the producer and artistic director of the Intimate Theatre described Strindberg's attitude to children in his book *Five years with August Strindberg*: "I don't think I have ever seen anyone who was as good to children as Strindberg. He played shops with his landlady's little daughter, weighed the various things, haggled about the price and finally paid up – in a very serious and dignified manner."

At the other extreme, death is never far away in any of these five plays. Even in THUNDER IN THE AIR we get a foretaste of it: ". . . come the evenings, carriages came and went, always fetching something or other. It took me two years before I realized that the flat

was being used as a nursing home and that the carriages were
collecting corpses in the night!" In AFTER THE FIRE practically all
the characters are involved in the business of death. The stone-mason,
the landlady of The Last Nail, the hearse driver, the florist. Death is
big business in AFTER THE FIRE.

In THE GHOST SONATA a murder has been committed before the
play begins and the guilty party, Mr Hummel appears the most moral
character in the whole play. Similarly, towards the end, when the
Student bares his soul to the Hyacinth girl, she collapses and dies
under the weight of so much emotion. One kills to conceal a crime
and another kills by telling the truth. THE PELICAN starts with the
smell of carbolic acid and a reminder of the recent death of the head
of the household. At the end, the young brother and sister perish in a
fire which is a symbolic cleansing of the spirit. In THE BLACK
GLOVE, finally, the wise old man who has spent his whole life
looking for the meaning of the universe, neglecting his wife and child
into the bargain, dies humbled but reconciled with his Maker. Death
is present in the sound of hearses, in the smell of carbolic acid, in the
spectacular vision of crackling fire, in the shape of funeral wreaths and
the fortifying drink at The Last Nail and finally it subsides, like a
musical coda, into a peaceful sleep in THE BLACK GLOVE.

Strindberg was obviously trying to get to terms with old age and
death when he wrote these five plays, but I believe they are also a
statement, however oblique, about the class system. It is no
coincidence that the Baker in THUNDER IN THE AIR, Opus 1,
occupies the space below stairs, that he harvests the fruits of the earth
and makes bread and jam while the wealthy people upstairs are trying
to pass the time of day with walks along the avenue, piano-playing,
chess and embroidery. The baker whose daughter runs off with the
young gentleman upstairs, appears not to understand what is going on
around him but I wonder whether Strindberg perhaps is reminding us
of Jean's lines in MISS JULIE. "To us love is like a game, something
we do when we've finished work, but we haven't got all day and all
night like you!"

The baker is busy supplying the basic food, earning a basic living. In
THE BLACK GLOVE it is the caretaker, again in the basement who
is in charge of all the machinery in the cellar – the central heating, the
electricity, the lift. He switches his buttons on and off and plays god
to all the families in 'The House of Babel', himself neglected and
forgotten but indispensable to the wealthy families above stairs.

Everyone pours out their heart to him and he listens and comforts and offers sensible down-to-earth advice.

In AFTER THE FIRE Strindberg gives the opening lines to a bricklayer. It is a very strong sympathetic portrait of an artisan, written at a time when the working-class was mostly portrayed as stupid or comical on the stage. All the workmen in AFTER THE FIRE go about their business as usual while the middle-class characters are whining and showing signs of nostalgia and guilt. Bricks and mortar versus illusions and lies. The milkmaid in THE GHOST SONATA, symbolically, gives the Student some water. In THE PELICAN the Nurse leaves the doomed household after an unprecedented tirade against the family. She complains of poor heating and lack of food and she ends facing her mistress defiantly: "Your turn will come too."

The well-off characters in these five plays all have to suffer. In THUNDER IN THE AIR, The Man's polished exterior crumbles when confronted with the raw passion of his erstwhile wife; in AFTER THE FIRE, the Stranger exposes the lies, past and present, to his brother who has tried to cheat the system but is doubly punished when his wife not only forgets to pay the premium in time but sees her lover instead. Cuckolded and ruined, he is brought down. In THE GHOST SONATA it is the arrogance of Mr Hummel which is finally challenged but also the whole carefully structured bourgeois family disintegrates before our very eyes. Strindberg holds up a distorting mirror to his characters and strips them of honours, class, dreams and beliefs.

In THE PELICAN, the mother indirectly killed her husband, robbed her children of food and nourishment and deceived her own daughter when she took her son-in-law as her lover. She too has to die, but first she must hear the painful truth about herself. This play which has so often been described as Strindberg's most vitriolic attack on women is, according to his eldest daughter Karin, a self-portrait. It is he, Strindberg himself, who is the vampire, who uses other people for his writings, it is he who has neglected and wrongly accused his spouse, it is he who in his old age is wooing another young woman, (in this case, Fanny Falkner the young actress to whom he was briefly engaged while writing this play.)

The Mother in THE PELICAN is the most awful self-portrait that Strindberg ever wrote. It is a bitter, cynical play and seems to be

most effective when played in a starkly realistic way, rather than in a
style which over-emphasizes the symbolic and supernatural aspects.
Strindberg himself called for a white set, clinically white. The contrast
between the light set and the dark emotions is then heightened and
the rocking-chair that moves by itself takes on a more sinister
significance.

In THE BLACK GLOVE the target is the rich young wife who does
not know what to do with her time and money; her only weakness is
her little daughter who is taken away from her temporarily by the
house sprites so as to teach her a lesson. The Student in THE
GHOST SONATA dreams of "having a flat on the fourth floor with
a young wife, two beautiful little children and a private income of
20,000 a year . . ." the very picture of the couple in THE BLACK
GLOVE in fact, but of whom the Old man in Opus 5 says "They're
too well-off, that's the whole trouble. The husband doesn't do
anything for a living . . ."

Kierkegaard, the Danish philosopher who meant so much to
Strindberg throughout his life, greatly influenced him in these
chamber plays too. The idea of 'repetition' (*gjentagelse*), is a well-
known Kierkegaard concept. Through repetition a pattern gradually
emerges in these five plays: the truth-seeking old men, the passionate
young women, the innocent girls, the saint-like children and the
dependable plodding working people. The main character in many of
the plays returns to a place where he has been intensely happy or
unhappy once, he looks for familiar points of contact, old grooves or he
tries to solve the mystery of life, but his return, his repetition only
becomes valuable when memory is rekindled by strong emotions.

This complicated pattern of humanity is depicted with a spice of
surrealism in THE PELICAN, some grotesque antics in THE
GHOST SONATA and pure fantasy in THE BLACK GLOVE.
Together they make up Strindberg's vision of a disjointed world, a
world where the tables are turned and the accuser becomes the
accused, the victim the perpetrator. Added to this basically pessimistic
view of life is a very personal brand of Christianity which Strindberg
had arrived at after his Inferno crisis in Paris in the nineties. Again it
is Kierkegaard and Swedenborg who pointed him in a special
direction. Kierkegaard was convinced that a person needs to
experience despair in order to find the meaning of life. About
Swedenborg, Strindberg said: "He has shown me the only path to
salvation, to seek out the demons in their dens within myself, and to

kill them through repentance." Despair and repentance run like two dominant threads through this weave.

There are other recurring *leitmotifs*; apparitions, like the milkmaid in THE GHOST SONATA, Gerda who appears like a ghost in a flash of lightning on her first entrance, the little people in THE BLACK GLOVE who are invisible but real because "You cannot touch the rainbow, but it's real all the same, so is the mirage when you're in the desert or at sea." In THE PELICAN the rocking-chair moves mysteriously by itself.

Illegitimacy also plays an important part in many of Strindberg's plays. The main characters in both AFTER THE FIRE and THE GHOST SONATA have fathered children out of wedlock. In THE BLACK GROVE, finally, we find many echoes of all the other chamber plays.

At the centre of the action there is often a hero who peels off layer after layer of lies until the people are unmasked and vulnerable, but in revealing pretence and hypocrisy he also brings chaos in his wake. Mr Hummel in THE GHOST SONATA has been abroad for many years when he returns to his old sweetheart with whom he has an illegitimate daughter. His ardently moral attitude is juxtaposed with his own lies and falsehood. In THE BLACK GLOVE it is the supernatural creatures who take on the role of prosecutors and in THUNDER IN THE AIR it is the brother, the visitor who straddles the various groups and tries to bring peace and harmony. In the more claustrophobic play THE PELICAN the drunken son is entrusted with this task.

Beneath the mask of respectability in these middle-class households are hidden a wealth of sins and crimes: alcoholism (THE PELICAN), fraud (THE GHOST SONATA and AFTER THE FIRE) adultery (THUNDER IN THE AIR, THE PELICAN, THE GHOST SONATA, AFTER THE FIRE) murder (THE GHOST SONATA) arson (AFTER THE FIRE). Clearly, with so much unsettled business between the various protagonists it is not surprising that Strindberg frequently refers to 'settling the accounts'. The final settlement eludes them however, and as a counterpoint to this fruitless striving for peace Strindberg introduces an illogical and sometimes bizarre language in these plays. He had a special reason for this: "The aborted intentions are to remain because they give a realistic effect as life is full of abandoned plans, ideas, projects which serve as fillers in people's conversations and at the same time create pools of energy."

Strindberg wrote the first four chamber plays in the spring of 1907. When the theatre finally opened with THE PELICAN in November 1907 the refurbishment had cost 45,000 *kronor* (£4,500). Strindberg himself put up a quarter of the sum and in order to pay the first month's rent he pawned his Occult Diary. He also had to guarantee the actors four months' salary. He personally supervised the work every morning before he took his daily walk. The theatre, which held 161 people and had fifteen rows of seats, was only open for three years. They were agonizing, often impecunious years and many times the company were on the brink of bankruptcy. On one such occasion Strindberg wrote an imploring letter to his publisher, begging for a loan but the answer was merciless:

"I regret that I must stay firm about my decision not to grant you a loan. As I informed you before, I have no interest in theatre in general, nor in the Intimate Theatre in particular. Yours faithfully, K.O. Bonnier"

They were saved from ruin that time by the intervention of one of the royal princes who also happened to be a painter, but in 1910 the financial difficulties became too great and the theatre closed for good. Strindberg never wrote another play after that.

In an ideal world, I would like to see these five plays performed in repertoire, using the same set, starting with the autumn play, Opus 1 where the action takes place both outside and inside the building, proceeding to Opus 5, THE BLACK GLOVE which also uses the whole building and takes place at Christmas, then on to THE PELICAN which is confined to a claustrophobic flat that goes up in flames; this leads naturally on to the burnt house in AFTER THE FIRE early in the spring, finishing in a surreal landscape in THE GHOST SONATA. With a dozen actors, an imaginative set and trimmed versions of the plays it could be a riveting experience.

EIVOR MARTINUS

Opus 1
THUNDER IN THE AIR

THUNDER IN THE AIR had its first production in this translation at the Gate Theatre, London in 1989. The cast was as follows:

THE MAN   Derek Smith

KARL FREDRIK   George Pensotti

MR. STARCK   Joseph Brady

AGNES   Maria Brown

LOUISE   Rebecca Saire

GERDA   Kim Thomson

DIRECTOR   Derek Martinus

CHARACTERS

THE MAN   (A retired civil servant)

KARL FREDRIK   (Here known as The Brother or The Consul)

MR STARCK   (Baker)

AGNES   (His daughter)

LOUISE   (Related to The Man and The Brother)

GERDA   (The Man's divorced wife)

MR FISCHER   (Gerda's present husband [non-speaking part])

ICEMAN

POSTMAN

LAMP-LIGHTER

ERRAND BOY

Scene One: The exterior of an apartment block

Scene Two: The interior

Scene Three: The exterior

SCENE ONE

The stage represents the exterior of an apartment block. The windows are surrounded by ornamental stonework. In the centre a low door leads into a yard, but it also serves as the entrance to Mr Starck's bakery. By the right-hand corner there is a small flower bed and a post-box. The ground floor apartment has large windows opening out from an elegantly furnished dining-room. On the first floor we can glimpse four more windows, covered with red blinds which are lit up from inside. In front of the house a pavement with some trees. In the foreground a green bench and a gas lamp.

Mr Starck enters, bringing a chair with him; he places it on the pavement and sits down.

The Man is seated by the table in the dining-room. Behind him there is a green tiled stove with a built-in mantel-shelf, adorned with a large photograph, two candelabras and two vases of flowers. A young girl dressed in light-coloured clothes is serving at the table.

THE
BROTHER: *(Enters from left, knocks with his walking stick on the window-sill outside the dining-room.)* Soon finished?

THE MAN: I'll be with you in a minute.

THE
BROTHER: *(Notices the other man on the pavement.)* Good evening, Mr Starck. Still quite warm for this time of the year, don't you think? *(Sits down on the bench.)*

MR STARCK: Good evening, sir. Yes, it is, but it's what you might expect in August, I suppose. My wife and I have been making jam all day . . .

THE
BROTHER: Have you really? Has it been a good year for berries?

MR STARCK: Not too bad. We had a cold spring of course, but the summer has been hot and stifling . . . especially for us who had to stay behind in town.

THE
BROTHER: I came back from the country yesterday. When the evenings are drawing in you begin to miss the city.

MR STARCK: Me and my wife haven't even been outside the city this
summer. There's always so much to do, even when
business is slack. First we had the strawberries, then
the wild strawberries, the cherries and raspberries and
gooseberries and apples and then the whole autumn
harvest . . .

THE
BROTHER: By the way, Mr Starck, do you happen to know if this
property is up for sale?

MR STARCK: I don't think so.

THE
BROTHER: Are there many people living here at the moment?

MR STARCK: There are ten households, I think. That is if you count
the other side of the block as well. But people don't
know one another here. Everybody keeps to themselves
– it's as if they are hiding away from each other. I've
lived here for ten years now and during the first couple
of years our neighbours didn't make a sound all day
long, but come the evening – carriages came and went,
always fetching something or other. It took me two
years before I realised that the flat was being used as a
nursing home and that the carriages were collecting
corpses in the night!

THE
BROTHER: How awful!

MR STARCK: People call this the silent house.

THE
BROTHER: Yes, it makes sense. People here don't seem to have
much to say to each other.

MR STARCK: The house is not without its share of dramas, though.

THE
BROTHER: Tell me, Mr Starck, who lives in that apartment
directly above my brother?

MR STARCK: You mean the one with the red curtains? Well, the
previous tenant died at the beginning of summer and
then it stood unoccupied for a month after that, but
last week a new family moved in. I haven't seen them
yet and I don't know their name. In fact, they never
seem to put a foot outside the flat. Why do you ask?

THE
BROTHER: Oh, no special reason. It just struck me that those red
               blinds look as if they are about to be lifted to reveal
               some bloody . . . drama . . . there is just a shadow of a
               palm on the blind. Apart from that there never seems
               to be any movement behind them.

MR STARCK: Oh, I've seen crowds of people there late at night.

THE
BROTHER: Men or women?

MR STARCK: Both, I think. Well, I must get back to my pots and
               pans in the kitchen. *(Leaves through the low door.)*

THE MAN: *(In the dining-room, rises, lights a cigar, goes to the
               window, talks to his brother through the open window.)*
               I'll soon be with you. Louise is just going to sew a
               button on one of my gloves.

THE
BROTHER: Do you want to take a walk into town?

THE MAN: Maybe, yes. Who were you talking to just now?

THE
BROTHER: The baker.

THE MAN: Oh yes, he's a nice fellow. He was my only friend here
               this summer, as a matter of fact.

THE
BROTHER: And you really spent every evening indoors throughout
               the whole summer?

THE MAN: Yes. I can't stand the long light evenings. It's different
               in the country, of course. It must be beautiful there in
               the evenings, but in town it seems to be against the
               laws of nature, somehow. I look forward to the time
               when they light the gas lamps again. Then I can take a
               real evening walk. It is so relaxing and it helps you go
               to sleep more easily. *(Louise hands over his glove.)*
               Thank you, my dear. You can leave the windows open.
               There are no mosquitoes about tonight. *(To his
               brother.)* I am coming now.

               *A moment later, the Man comes into the yard, puts a
               letter in the box, walks to the front and sits down
               beside his brother.*

THE
BROTHER: Why do you stay in town when you could be in the
            country?

THE MAN: To be honest with you I don't know. I suppose I've
            become immobilized, chained to this place by all its
            memories. This is the only place where I can find peace
            and where I feel safe. It's interesting to look at one's
            apartment from the outside, don't you think? I always
            imagine someone else walking about in there . . . just
            think, I've lived here for ten years now . . .

THE
BROTHER: Is it really ten?

THE MAN: Yes, ten. *(Pause)* Why is it that time always seems to
            drag on indefinitely when you're in the middle of life,
            but when you look at things in retrospect, time seems
            to have passed so quickly. *(Short pause.)* This house
            was quite new when I moved in; I even watched them
            putting down the parquet floor in the drawing-room
            and I was here when they painted the panels and the
            doors. *She* chose the wallpapers and I haven't replaced
            them since. *(Short pause.)* Well, that's all in the past.
            Mr Starck and I have lived here longer than anyone
            else. His life is not entirely undramatic either . . . He is
            the sort of person who never makes a success of
            anything. He's always getting into trouble. I have
            suffered with him through all his worries and I have
            carried his burdens as well as my own.

THE
BROTHER: Is he a . . . heavy drinker?

THE MAN: Oh no. No, he's not like that at all, but he lacks
            ambition. He and I know the whole history of this
            apartment block. We've seen the newly-weds arrive in
            their horse and carriage and we've seen others leave in
            their hearses. And you see that letter-box over there
            . . . that has received many a secret, you know.

THE
BROTHER: I heard that one of the tenants died this summer.

THE MAN: Yes, he was a bank manager. He died of typhoid. His
            flat stood empty for over a month; first to leave was the

coffin, then the widow and her children and last of all the furniture . . .

THE
BROTHER: Did he live in the flat above you?

THE MAN: Yes, over there . . . where the lights are on. There are some new people living there now, but I haven't met them yet.

THE
BROTHER: You haven't seen them either?

THE MAN: I never ask about the other tenants. I listen to gossip, but I refuse to get involved because I enjoy the quiet life of old age.

THE
BROTHER: Old age, yes. I must admit I rather enjoy growing old. You're nearing the end of the run.

THE MAN: I agree. I'm just in the process of settling my accounts with people and I've already started to pack, so to speak, for the ultimate journey. Solitude need not be such a bad thing; as long as you haven't got any creditors you're free to come and go as you please, to think and eat and sleep and go shopping just as you like.

              One of the blinds is half lifted and we glimpse a woman's dress behind it.

THE
BROTHER: There is someone moving about up there. Did you see?

              The blind is pulled down again.

THE MAN: Yes, very mysterious. But it is worse at night. Sometimes they play music, but not very good music. And sometimes they play cards. And at the crack of dawn, carriages are coming and going . . . but I don't make a fuss because I always find that counterproductive, don't you? They're likely to retaliate and nobody ever changes anyway. You're often better off not knowing what's going on.

              A gentleman, wearing a dinner-jacket but no hat, enters with a pile of letters which he posts in the letter-box. Then he exits hurriedly.

THE
BROTHER: Did you see all those letters he had?

THE MAN: They looked like circulars.

THE
BROTHER: Who was it?

THE MAN: It must have been the new tenant on the first floor . . .

THE
BROTHER: Was it? What do you make of him, judging by his
            appearance I mean?

THE MAN: I don't know. A musician, perhaps. A music hall artist?
            A gambler? A bit of a Casanova? A bit of everything in
            fact.

THE
BROTHER: With that pale complexion you would expect him to
            have black hair, but it seemed to be brown, so either
            he's dyed it or he's wearing a wig. And wearing a
            dinner-jacket at home! He must be short of clothes.
            And did you see the way he moved his hands when he
            put those letters in the box? It looked like "shuffle and
            deal, shuffle and deal . . ."

            We hear a waltz being played on the first floor.

THE MAN: Nothing but waltzes.

THE
BROTHER: Maybe they're running a dancing school.

THE MAN: But it's nearly always the same old waltz.

THE
BROTHER: *(Listens for a moment.)* What is it called now again?

THE MAN: "Pluie d'or." I know it by heart.

THE
BROTHER: Didn't you use to play it at home?

THE MAN: Yes, that one and "Alcazar."

            *Louise can be seen in the dining-room, putting some
            glasses back on the sideboard.*

THE
BROTHER: Are you still satisfied with Louise?

THE MAN: Very.

THE
BROTHER: Isn't she thinking of getting married soon?

THE MAN: Not that I know of.

THE
BROTHER: Has she got a "beau"?

THE MAN: Why do you ask?

THE
BROTHER: Maybe you've got designs on her yourself . . .

THE MAN: Me? No thank you! Last time I entered into marriage I
             was still comparatively young. And we soon had a
             child, as you know, but now I'm past that sort of thing
             and I only want to grow old in peace . . . Do you think
             I would enjoy having another master in my house and
             do you think I would like to lose my property and life
             and risk being dishonoured . . .

THE
BROTHER: Your life and property have never been at risk, as far as
             I know.

THE MAN: But I have been dishonoured, you mean?

THE
BROTHER: Didn't you know?

THE MAN: What do you mean?

THE
BROTHER: Yes, she dishonoured you, when she left . . .

THE MAN: So for the last five years my reputation has been sullied
             without my knowing it?

THE
BROTHER: Surely you knew?

THE MAN: No, I didn't. When I remarried a young girl, thirty
             years my junior, I realised that the age difference might
             become an obstacle one day so, although she consented
             happily to the marriage, I promised her that I would
             set her free as soon as my age were to prove a serious
             problem. Well, our child was born within a decent

passage of time and we didn't want any more children. When my daughter started to grow away from me I began to feel superfluous so I left. I took a boat to the mainland – we were staying on an island in the archipelago at the time, if you remember. And that was the end of that. I kept my promise and saved further embarrassment. What more could I do?

THE
BROTHER: Yes, but she felt deceived all the same, because she had been the one who had wanted to leave. That is why she came with all those accusations behind your back.

THE MAN: Did she never consider herself guilty in any way?

THE
BROTHER: No, she lays all the blame on you.

THE MAN: That's alright then.

Pause.

THE
BROTHER: Do you know what happened to her and your child after you left?

THE MAN: I never tried to find out. After having lived through the horrors of the divorce proceedings, I considered the whole matter dead and buried, but as this apartment only retained the beautiful memories of our relationship I saw no point in moving away from here. Thanks for your interesting information, though.

THE
BROTHER: What information?

THE MAN: You said that she doesn't hold herself responsible. That must mean that she blames me.

THE
BROTHER: I think you're under a great delusion, my dear brother.

THE MAN: Maybe you're right. A clear conscience, relatively clear anyway, has always been like a diver's suit to me; it enables me to reach the depths without any danger of losing my breath. *(Gets up.)* Just think . . . I got out of that situation unscathed! And now it's all over. Shall we take a walk along the avenue?

THE BROTHER:	Yes, why not? And watch the first gas lamp being lit.
THE MAN:	I think we'll see the moon tonight. The August moon.
THE BROTHER:	Yes and I believe it's a full moon even . . .
THE MAN:	*(Talks to Louise who is in the dining-room.)* Louise, please give me my walking stick. The lightweight one.
LOUISE:	*(Handing him his stick through the window.)* Here you are.
THE MAN:	Thank you, my dear. You'll turn the lights out when you've finished in the dining-room, won't you? We'll be gone for a while. I am not quite sure how long we'll be.

The two men exit left. Louise remains by the window.

MR STARCK:	*(Entering through the low door.)* Good evening, Miss Louise. Still hot and sticky, don't you think? Have the two gentlemen gone?
LOUISE:	Yes, they've gone for a walk down by the avenue. It's the first time this summer that the master has gone out in the evening.
MR STARCK:	When you get to our age you'll appreciate the hour of dusk. It hides so many flaws . . . both in ourselves and others . . . do you know, my dear . . . my wife is going blind but she doesn't want to have an operation. Because there is nothing worth looking at, she says. And sometimes she even wishes that she were going deaf.
LOUISE:	You feel like that sometimes.
MR STARCK:	You lead such a quiet and beautiful life in there. And you're not short of money, no worries . . . I never hear any raised voices from you or any doors being slammed. Perhaps it's even a little too quiet for a young lady like you?
LOUISE:	Good Lord, no. I love this peaceful existence and the dignified atmosphere here. No one says too much and people don't bring up any unpleasant or trivial subjects . . .

MR STARCK: And you never entertain?

LOUISE: No, the only caller is the consul. I've never come across such brotherly love in my life.

MR STARCK: Who is the eldest?

LOUISE: I don't know. It may be one or two years between them, or they may be twins in fact, because they always seem to treat each other with the utmost respect.

Agnes tries to sneak past Mr Starck.

MR STARCK: Where are you going, my girl?

AGNES: I was just going for a walk.

MR STARCK: Enjoy yourself then, girl, but don't be too long. *(Agnes leaves.)* Do you think your uncle still misses his wife and daughter terribly?

LOUISE: No, I don't think so. He may miss them occasionally but he certainly doesn't wish them to come back. They live on in his memory. He only keeps the beautiful moments, you see . . .

MR STARCK: But he must worry about his daughter sometimes . . .

LOUISE: Yes, he must wonder whether his wife has remarried, and who the stepfather is in that case . . .

MR STARCK: I've heard that his wife didn't want any alimony at first but after five years she sent along a solicitor with a bill for several thousand . . .

LOUISE: *(Curtly)* I don't know anything about that.

MR STARCK: Anyway, she is probably more lovely in his memory now . . .

An errand boy appears with a basket full of wine bottles.

ERRAND BOY: Excuse me, does Mr Fischer live here?

LOUISE: Mr Fischer? Not as far as I know.

MR STARCK: Could it be the man on the first floor? Try the door up there, the entrance is around the corner.

ERRAND BOY: *(Leaving)* First floor, thank you.

LOUISE: All those bottles will mean another sleepless night.

MR STARCK: What sort of people are they? Why do they never show
                   themselves in daylight?

LOUISE: I think they must be using the servants' door. I've
                   never seen them, but I have heard them alright.

MR STARCK: Yes, you can't avoid hearing them, with all those doors
                   banging and corks popping and all kinds of things
                   bashing and crashing . . .

LOUISE: They never open a window, not even in this heat.
                   Look, there was a flash of lightning. One, two, three
                   . . . No, just a false alarm. No thunder.

WOMAN'S
VOICE: *(From the basement.)* Aren't you going to come and help me
                   with the bottling?

MR STARCK: Coming, dear. We're making jam, you see. Coming,
                   coming. *(Exits)*

                   Louise remains by the open window.

THE
BROTHER: *(Enters slowly from the right.)* Has my brother come
                   back yet?

LOUISE: No, I thought he was with you.

THE
BROTHER: He went to make a telephone call and he asked me to
                   walk ahead. Well, I suppose he won't be long. What's
                   that? *(Bends down to pick up a postcard.)* "Boston club
                   after midnight." Signed "Fischer". Who is this
                   Fischer? Do you know?

LOUISE: There was a lad here just now with some wine. He was
                   looking for a Mr Fischer too, on the first floor.

THE
BROTHER: The Fischers on the first floor! With the red blind
                   which shines like the red light above the tobacconist's
                   at night. I think you've got bad company in the house.

LOUISE: What does "Boston club" mean?

THE
BROTHER: It could be something quite innocent, but in this case
I'm not so sure. How did the postcard turn up here?
Oh, the man in the dinner-jacket must have dropped it
just now. I'll post it then. Fischer? . . . Fischer . . . I'd
like to ask you something. Does my brother never talk
about the past?

LOUISE: Never with me anyway.

THE
BROTHER: Miss Louise, may I ask you . . .

We hear the sound of milk churns in the distance.

LOUISE: Excuse me, the evening milk has just arrived. I must go
and fetch it.

*She leaves. The milkmaid is seen on the right. She
walks across the stage.*

MR STARCK: *(Enters, takes off his white cap, panting.)* In and out like
a badger. It's terrible down there by the hot stove and
no evening breeze to cool you down either . . .

THE
BROTHER: I think rain is forecast. Look at the lightning. It's not
very nice down in town but it's peaceful enough up
here. No carriages rattling past and no trams. You
could almost imagine you're in the country.

MR STARCK: It may be peaceful alright, but it's a bit too quiet for
business. I may be a good baker and pastry-maker but
I'm certainly no good at selling, never have been and
don't seem to be able to learn either. Or maybe it's
something else . . . maybe I haven't got the inclination
for it. You see, as soon as someone as much as suspects
me of cheating I go all red in the face and then I get
angry. But I'm too old for that sort of anger now. It's
wearing, everything is wearing.

THE
BROTHER: Why don't you try your hand at something else then?

MR STARCK: Nobody wants me.

THE
BROTHER: Have you tried?

MR STARCK: There is no point.

THE
BROTHER: I see.

> *A drawn-out grunting noise is heard from the floor above.*

MR STARCK: What in heaven's name are they up to? Are they killing each other or what?

THE
BROTHER: I don't like this unknown thing that's come into the apartment block. It looms like a big red thunder cloud . . . what kind of people are they up there? Where do they come from and what do they want?

MR STARCK: It's dangerous to sniff around in other people's business. But you can't help getting involved, can you?

THE
BROTHER: Do you know anything about them?

MR STARCK: No, I don't know anything.

> *Someone is screaming in the distance.*

THE
BROTHER: There it is again.

MR STARCK: *(Leaving slowly.)* I don't want to get involved.

> *Gerda enters, her hair hanging loose. She is in an agitated state. The Brother walks towards her, they recognize each other, she shies away.*

THE
BROTHER: So it was you, after all.

GERDA: Yes.

THE
BROTHER: How did you come to live here? Can't you even let my poor brother enjoy his retirement in peace?

GERDA: *(Distraught)* They misinformed me. I thought he had moved. It wasn't my fault . . .

THE BROTHER:	You don't need to be afraid of me. Don't be afraid of me, Gerda. Is there any way I can help you? What's going on up there anyway?
GERDA:	He hit me.
THE BROTHER:	Is your little daughter with you?
GERDA:	Yes.
THE BROTHER:	So she has a stepfather now?
GERDA:	Yes.
THE BROTHER:	Put your hair up and calm yourself and I'll try and sort this out, but please keep my brother out of this . . .
GERDA:	I suppose he hates me?
THE BROTHER:	No, can't you see how well he looks after your old flower-bed here? He carried the potting mixture here himself. Don't you recognize your blue gentian and your mignonette, your very own roses, Malmaison and Merveille de Lyon which he grafted on himself. He worships the memory of you and your daughter.
GERDA:	Where is he now?
THE BROTHER:	He is just buying an evening paper and when he comes back you'll see he'll enter the house from the courtyard over there. Then he'll sit down in the dining-room and read the paper. So if you keep still he won't notice you. But you really ought to go back upstairs.
GERDA:	I can't do that. I can't go back to that man . . .
THE BROTHER:	Who is he anyway? What does he do for a living?
GERDA:	He used to be a singer.
THE BROTHER:	Used to be . . . what is he now then? Has he got a gambling club upstairs or something?

GERDA: *(Hesitant)* Yes.

THE
BROTHER: And the child . . . I suppose he uses the child as a
              decoy?

GERDA: Don't say that.

THE
BROTHER: But this is awful!

GERDA: You make it sound worse than it is.

THE
BROTHER: We must treat obscenity with kid gloves, you mean?
              Why did you bring shame on my brother and why did
              you have to make me into your accomplice? I was naive
              enough to believe you and I defended your unjust
              cause against his.

GERDA: You forget that he was too old for me.

THE
BROTHER: He wasn't too old then. The child is proof of that.
              When he asked you to marry him, he also asked if you
              wanted to have a child. And he promised to release you
              if his age were ever to be an embarrassment to you.

GERDA: He deserted me and that was a terrible insult.

THE
BROTHER: Not for you. Your youth protected you . . .

GERDA: He should have let me leave.

THE
BROTHER: Why? Why would you prefer to bring shame on him
              instead?

GERDA: One of us had to bear the blame.

THE
BROTHER: What strange reasoning. You have succeeded in
              annihilating him. And to think that you've involved me
              in all this. How can we repair the damage we've
              caused?

GERDA: We can't, unless it is at my expense.

THE
BROTHER: I don't follow you. Why are you so full of hate? Forget
              the question of honour and blame for a moment . . .
              what is best for the child?

GERDA: The child is mine. She belongs to me now and my
              present husband is her legitimate father . . .

THE
BROTHER: You're a hard woman, Gerda. And you've become
              scruffy and coarse as well. Shhh, here he comes.

              *The Man enters from left with a newspaper in his
              hand. He goes in to his apartment, deep in thought.
              The Brother and Gerda stand quite still, concealed by
              the corner of the house. The Man sits down in his
              dining-room, starts reading the paper.*

GERDA: It's him!

THE
BROTHER: Come and look at your old home. See how he has kept
              everything the way you arranged it once. Don't be
              afraid, he can't see us in the dark. He's got the light in
              his eyes, you see.

GERDA: How he has lied to me . . .

THE
BROTHER: In what way?

GERDA: Why, he hasn't aged at all. He just grew tired of me,
              that's all. Look at his collar and his cravat, both the
              latest fashion. I suppose he has a mistress too.

THE
BROTHER: Yes, he's got a portrait of her on the mantelshelf
              between the two candlesticks.

GERDA: Has he? That's a photo of me and my daughter! Does
              he still love me then?

THE
BROTHER: He loves the memory of you.

GERDA: How strange. *(The Man stops reading, looks out of the
              window.)* He is looking straight at us.

THE
BROTHER: Keep still!

GERDA: He is looking me straight in the eye.

THE
BROTHER: Stand still. He can't see you.

GERDA: He looks quite lifeless . . .

THE
BROTHER: I told you – you annihilated him.

GERDA: Why do you say things like that?

> *The Brother and Gerda are illuminated by a sudden*
> *flash of lightning. The Man gets up, looks upset.*
> *Gerda runs away, hides behind the corner of the house.*

THE MAN: Karl Fredrik! *(Goes to the window.)* Are you alone out
there? I thought . . . are you really alone?

THE
BROTHER: As you can see.

THE MAN: It's so stuffy . . . the scent of flowers is giving me a
headache. I'll just finish reading this article. *(Resumes
his place by the table.)*

THE
BROTHER: *(To Gerda.)* Now . . . do you want me to accompany
you upstairs?

GERDA: Maybe. But there's bound to be arguments and trouble
of all sorts.

THE
BROTHER: We must get the child away from him. I'll think of a
way. I did train as a lawyer, after all.

GERDA: Only for the child's sake, mind you. I'll show you the
way. *(They leave.)*

THE MAN: *(From the dining-room.)* Karl Fredrik! Come and play a
game of chess with me, please. Karl Fredrik!

SCENE TWO

The dining-room. At the back there is a tiled stove. To the left an open door leads into the pantry. To the right a door leads to the hall. On the left-hand side there is a sideboard with a telephone on it, to the right a piano and a grandfather clock.

Louise enters.

THE MAN: Where did my brother get to?

LOUISE: *(Uneasy)* He was outside just now. I don't think he could have gone very far.

THE MAN: There is a terrible noise coming from upstairs. They are tramping about, pulling out drawers as if they were in the middle of moving. Maybe they're running away from something. Oh, I wish you knew how to play chess, Louise.

LOUISE: I can play a little.

THE MAN: All you need to know is how to set out the various pieces. Sit down, my dear. *(He organizes the board.)* Look, they are making such a commotion upstairs that the chandeliers are rattling. And downstairs Mr Starck is stoking his fires. I think I'd better move away from here.

LOUISE: Yes, I think you'd better. You've stayed here far too long already.

THE MAN: Why?

LOUISE: It's not good to get too wrapped up in one's memories.

THE MAN: And why not? With the passing of time, all memories emerge as beautiful.

LOUISE: But you could live on another twenty years, perhaps. Memories pale in the end and maybe they'll even change colour one day.

THE MAN: How wise you are, my child. Your pawn first. Not the queen because then you'll be in check in two moves.

LOUISE: I think I'll start with the knight . . .

THE MAN: Just as risky, I'm afraid.

LOUISE: I'll start with the knight anyway.

THE MAN: Alright, then I'll move the bishop . . .

             Mr Starck appears in the hall, carrying a tray.

LOUISE: Mr Starck is here with some fresh bread. He's as quiet
             as a mouse.

             *Louise gets up and walks out to the hall, takes the tray
             and puts it down in the pantry.*

THE MAN: Well, Starck, how is Mrs Starck keeping?

MR STARCK: Thank you for asking, sir. It's her eyes as usual, you
             know . . .

THE MAN: Have you seen my brother?

MR STARCK: I think he's walking around outside.

THE MAN: Has he got someone with him?

MR STARCK: No, I don't think so.

THE MAN: It is some time since you saw this flat now, isn't it?

MR STARCK: Yes, as a matter of fact, it is exactly ten years ago I was
             in here last.

THE MAN: That's when you delivered our wedding cake. Well, has
             there been much of a change, do you think?

MR STARCK: No, everything is just as it was . . . The palms have
             grown, of course. Yes, just as it was . . .

THE MAN: And nothing will change until you come here with the
             cake for my funeral. When you get past a certain age,
             nothing really changes, everything around you stops,
             but you move on all the same like a toboggan down a
             steep slope . . .

MR STARCK: That's just how it is.

THE MAN: And it's nice and quiet like this. No love affairs, no
             friends, just a little company to break the silence.
             People appear really human and they don't make any
             emotional demands on you. In the end you become
             loose like an old tooth and fall out painlessly. Take
             Louise for instance, a beautiful young girl whose very
             presence fills me with joy, like when you look at a work

of art without necessarily wanting to own it. Nothing spoils our relationship. And my brother and I meet like two old gentlemen who never get too close or intimate with each other. By keeping a neutral position you gain a certain distance and at a distance we all appear a little more to our advantage. In other words, I'm content with my old age and my peaceful existence. Louise!

LOUISE: *(In the doorway.)* I've just taken in the laundry and I must count it.

THE MAN: Well, Mr Starck, don't you want to sit down and have a chat? Perhaps you play chess?

MR STARCK: No, I can't leave my pots and pans any longer, and at eleven o'clock I've got to light the baking oven. But thanks for asking me all the same . . .

THE MAN: If you see my brother, would you please ask him to come and keep me company.

MR STARCK: I will. Of course I will. *(Exits)*

           The Man moves the chess pieces on his own for a while, then he rises and paces up and down; sits down by the piano, plays a couple of chords, gets up and paces up and down again.

THE MAN: Louise, can't you leave the laundry for the moment and do that later?

LOUISE: *(In the same doorway as before.)* No, I'm afraid the laundry woman is in a hurry. Her family is waiting for her . . .

THE MAN: I see. *(Sits down by the table, taps his fingers against the table-top, tries to read the newspaper, but gives up; strikes a couple of matches and blows them out again; looks at the grandfather clock. He seems for a moment to lapse into reverie. There is a knock on the front door.)* Karl Fredrik, is that you?

POSTMAN: It's the postman. *(Enters)* Excuse me, but the door was open . . .

THE MAN: Any letters for me?

POSTMAN: Just a postcard. *(Hands it over and leaves.)*

THE MAN: *(Reads the card.)* Mr Fischer again. "Boston club". It is
            the man upstairs! The man in the dinner-jacket . . .
            with the white hands. And he is inviting me . . . what
            an insult. I must move away from here. Fischer . . .
            (Tears the card. He is lost in thought for a moment.
            Another knock on the front door.) Karl Fredrik, is that
            you?

ICEMAN: *(Off-stage)* It's only the iceman.

THE MAN: Lovely to get some ice in this heat. But handle the
            bottles carefully, won't you? Could you tilt the ice so I
            can hear those melting drops . . . they're like my water-
            clock measuring out the time, the drawn-out time.
            (Pause) Hey, where do you get the ice from by the
            way? Has he gone? Everyone disappears, everyone goes
            home . . . to seek company, exchange a few words . . .
            (Long pause.) Karl Fredrik, is that you?

                Chopin's Fantasie Impromptu Opus 66, is played on a
                piano.

THE MAN: *(Listening, looks at the ceiling.)* Who is that playing my
            impromptu? *(He covers his eyes with his hands and*
            listens.)

                The Brother enters from the hall.

THE MAN: Karl Fredrik, is that you?

                The music stops.

THE
BROTHER: Yes, it's me.

THE MAN: Where have you been all this time?

THE
BROTHER: I had some business to sort out. Have you been alone?

THE MAN: Yes, of course. Come and play chess with me now.

THE
BROTHER: I'd rather have a talk. And I'm sure you could do with
            a bit of vocal exercise too.

THE MAN: True, true, but we always end up talking about the past
            . . .

THE
BROTHER: And forget the present . . .

THE MAN: There is no such thing as the present. What we call the
            present is just a vacuum; there is the future and the
            past, but I'd rather have the future because there lies
            our hope.

THE
BROTHER: *(At the table.)* Hope for what?

THE MAN: Change.

THE
BROTHER: I see. Does that mean you've had enough of your
            peaceful retirement?

THE MAN: Maybe.

THE
BROTHER: That means yes. And if it were possible to choose
            between your present solitude and your past . . .

THE MAN: No ghosts, thank you.

THE
BROTHER: What about your memories then?

THE MAN: They are no spectres. They are like poems of certain
            events; but if the people of the past were to materialize
            again then they would appear like ghosts.

THE
BROTHER: Which of the two, the woman or the child is your most
            treasured memory?

THE MAN: They are both as precious. I can't make any distinction
            between them. That's why I did not want to fight for
            custody.

THE
BROTHER: But was it the right thing to do? Didn't you consider
            the possibility of a stepfather?

THE MAN: I didn't think so much in those days. But I must admit
            that I have brooded over the matter lately.

THE
BROTHER: A stepfather who might assault your child, perhaps
            even abuse her sexually?

THE MAN: *(Aghast at first, then he is distracted.)* Shhh . . .

THE
BROTHER: Did you hear anything?

THE MAN: Yes, I thought I heard those familiar little steps, like
              the tripping steps I used to hear in the corridor when
              she came to see me. I think the child was the greatest
              treasure, after all. Watching that courageous little
              creature who was not afraid of anything, who did not
              suspect any treachery in life and who didn't keep any
              secrets. *(Pause)* I remember the first time she came
              across people's wickedness. She had just caught sight of
              another beautiful little girl in the park and she walked
              up to her with outstretched arms, ready to embrace the
              stranger. The beautiful little girl returned her kiss by
              biting her cheek and sticking her tongue out. You
              should have seen my little Ann-Charlotte's expression.
              She was quite paralysed, not from the pain, but
              because she was horrified to see this abyss opening up
              before her, this abyss we call the human heart. I have
              experienced this kind of thing once too, when two
              beautiful eyes suddenly became hostile. I was so
              frightened that I had to look behind her to see if
              someone was hiding there. Her face was like a mask.
              But how did we get on to this subject? It must be the
              heat or the thunder in the air.

THE
BROTHER: You need company. Being on your own is making you
              gloomy. This summer in town seems to have depressed
              you.

THE MAN: It's only during the last couple of weeks I've felt like
              this; that person dying upstairs upset me and I've got
              involved in all Mr Starck's problems so now I find
              myself worrying about his finances, his wife's eyesight,
              his future . . . and recently I've also been dreaming
              about my little Ann-Charlotte . . . I dream that she is
              in some unknown danger, and just before I go to sleep
              . . . you know, when your hearing always seems to be
              more acute than normal, I hear her little steps, and
              once I even thought I heard her voice . . .

THE BROTHER:	Where is she then?
THE MAN:	Hmmm . . .
THE BROTHER:	If you were to meet her in the street by chance . . .
THE MAN:	I think I'd lose my senses or drop down dead. *(Pause)* Once when our sister was very young, I spent several years abroad, and when I finally returned home and stepped ashore from the steamer, a young girl came up to me and embraced me. The stranger had a penetrating gaze and her eyes expressed a horror at not being recognized. "It's me," she said again and again, before I realised who it was. That is roughly how I imagine the reunion with my daughter. Five years at that age is a long time. I may not even recognize her. Just imagine, *not recognizing my own child!* The same, but a complete stranger. I could not endure that. No, I'd rather keep my little four year-old here at my altar. As I remember her. *(Pause)* Is that you, Louise? Are you sorting out the linen cupboard? I like the smell of clean linen, it reminds me of . . . the housewife by the linen chest, the good fairy who looks after and restores her supplies, the mistress of the house who smooths over the rough surfaces with her iron and irons out the wrinkles, yes, the wrinkles . . . I think I'll . . . I'll go and write a letter. Do you want to stay here? I'll be back soon. *(Exits left.)*

    The Brother coughs.

GERDA:	*(In the hallway.)* Are you . . . *(The clock chimes.)* Oh, my God! That chime . . . I've carried it around with me for ten years now. This clock which never kept the time, but measured out the hours, the days and nights of five long years. *(Looks around.)* My piano . . . and my plants . . . the dining-table. He has looked after it well. It's polished like a shield. My sideboard with Eve and her knight in armour. Eve with her apples in the basket. And in the right-hand drawer, in the far corner there used to be a thermometer . . . *(Pause)* I wonder if it's still there . . . *(Pulls out the right-hand drawer.)* Yes, there it is.

THE
BROTHER: What does that signify?

GERDA: It became like a symbol of our relationship in the end.
               When we first got married this thermometer got left
               behind in this drawer. We meant to fix it outside the
               window and I promised to put it there, but then I
               forgot, and he promised to do it, but he forgot too, so
               we nagged each other about it and in the end I put it
               in this drawer in order to avoid further trouble. But I
               began to hate this thing and so did he. Do you realise
               what that meant? It meant that neither of us really
               believed in the permanence of our relationship. We
               revealed our true selves at once and didn't conceal our
               feelings of hostility. The first couple of months after we
               got married we were ready to take a leap in the dark,
               always prepared to break up. Like the thermometer . . .
               and here it is still. Up and down, changeable like the
               weather. *(She puts it aside and goes to the chessboard.)*
               My chessboard . . . which he bought to pass the time
               while we were waiting for the baby to arrive. Oh, that
               long wait. Who plays with him now?

THE
BROTHER: I do.

GERDA: Where is he now?

THE
BROTHER: He's in his study, writing a letter.

GERDA: And this is where he has spent the last five years?

THE
BROTHER: The last ten years. Five of them on his own.

GERDA: He loves being on his own.

THE
BROTHER: I think he may have had enough of it by now.

GERDA: Do you think he'll receive me?

THE
BROTHER: You can always try. You don't risk anything by trying.
               He is always courteous.

GERDA: I didn't make that table runner . . .

THE BROTHER:	He may ask questions about the child.
GERDA:	He must help me to find her. . . .
THE BROTHER:	Where do you think your husband has got to? And what is the reason for this running away?
GERDA:	He wanted to get away from this unpleasant neighbourhood, he said. And now he wants me to chase after him. He has taken Ann-Charlotte with him as hostage, he wants her to become a ballet dancer. Apparently she has shown some real talent in that field.
THE BROTHER:	The ballet? You must not tell my brother that. He hates everything to do with the theatre.
GERDA:	*(Sits down by the chessboard, starts moving the chess pieces abstractedly.)* The theatre . . . but I used to be on the stage, too.
THE BROTHER:	You!
GERDA:	Yes, I thought you . . . I accompanied my husband on the piano when he sang.
THE BROTHER:	Poor Gerda!
GERDA:	Why poor? I loved it.
THE BROTHER:	Now you've had enough, yes?
GERDA:	Now I look forward to some peace and quiet, being alone . . . with my daughter, of course.
THE BROTHER:	Shh . . . he is coming.
GERDA:	*(Gets up, ready to run away, sits down again.)* Oh!
THE BROTHER:	I'll leave you two alone. Don't plan ahead what you're going to say. One move leads to the next naturally, just like in chess.

GERDA: I worry most about his first reaction. I will be able to
                tell from his look whether I've changed to my
                advantage or disadvantage . . . if I've grown old and
                ugly . . .

THE
BROTHER: (By the door to the right.) If he thinks you have aged,
                he'll approach you more readily, but if he still finds
                you attractive then all hope is lost for him, and
                remember he is less critical than you think. Here he is.
                (The Man walks slowly past the open door to the pantry,
                carrying a letter in his hand. He then disappears for a
                moment and turns up in the hall area and exits.
                The Brother, still by the door on the right.) He went out
                to post a letter.

GERDA: I'll never manage to go through with this. How can I
                possibly ask him to help me with this divorce? No, I'll
                leave now. I am presuming too much.

THE
BROTHER: No, stay. You know he is the soul of honour and he
                will help you for the sake of the child.

GERDA: No, no.

THE
BROTHER: And he is the only one who can help you. (Exits)

THE MAN: (Enters quickly from the hall, nods in Gerda's direction,
                whom he mistakes for Louise, goes to the telephone and
                makes a call through the operator. In passing he addresses
                Gerda.) Are you ready? Let's start from the beginning
                again, Louise, from the beginning. (Gerda petrified,
                doesn't understand. The Man, with his back to Gerda,
                making his phone call.) Three six, please. Hello! Good
                evening, is that you, mother? . . . Yes, thank you.
                Louise is already waiting by the chessboard. She is a
                little tired after all the bustle today . . . Yes, that's all
                over now and everything is alright. Mere trifles . . .
                Too hot? Oh yes. There was thunder in the air but no
                flash of lightning. Just a false alarm . . . Oh, you mean
                the Fischers? Yes. But I think they are in the process
                of moving . . . No, I don't know any reason . . . I see.
                I see. Yes, it leaves at six fifteen and goes through the
                outer archipelago and it arrives, let me see now . . . at

eight twenty-five . . . Did you enjoy yourselves then?
. . . *(Laughs)* Yes, he's quite a fellow when he gets
going. What did Maria say about that? . . . How was
your summer then? . . . Not too bad. Louise has kept
me company. She's such a good-tempered girl. And
she's so kind too . . . No, thank you. *(Gerda begins to
understand, sits down, alarmed.)* My eyes? Well, I've
become a bit short-sighted, I suppose, but it's like Mrs
Starck says: there is nothing worth looking at anyway.
She'd prefer to go deaf as well. Deaf and blind. Our
new neighbours upstairs create pandemonium every
night. I think they must be running some gambling
club or . . . damn, we got cut off. It's because they're
listening in on the line. *(Louise appears in the hall, but
the Man doesn't see her. Gerda looks at Louise with a
mixture of admiration and dislike. Louise withdraws
through the right door. The Man, still on the telephone.)*
Are you still there? We were cut off, yes. Someone was
listening. Shall we say tomorrow at six fifteen then?
Thank you, the same to you. Yes, I will. Good-bye,
mother. *(Replaces the receiver. Louise has left. Gerda
stands in the middle of the room.)* Now then! *(Turns
round, sees Gerda and finally recognizes her, puts his
hand to his heart.)* Oh, my God, is it you? Was it you
and not Louise who was standing over there a minute
ago? *(Gerda doesn't answer. Faintly.)* How . . . did you
. . . get here?

GERDA: I'm sorry . . . I just happened to walk past and I
longed to see my old home again. The windows were
open and . . .

    Pause.

THE MAN: Well, do you think it has changed much?

GERDA: No, it's just the same, but something has come between
. . .

THE MAN: *(Ill-at-ease)* Are you happy . . . in your new life?

GERDA: Yes, it's as I expected.

THE MAN: And our daughter?

GERDA: She is growing and she is happy.

THE MAN: Then I won't ask any more questions. *(Pause)* Do you want anything from me, can I help you in any way?

GERDA: Thank you for asking but . . . I don't need anything. I can see that you're well too. *(Pause)* Do you want to see Ann-Charlotte?

> *Pause.*

THE MAN: I don't think so. Now that I know she's alright. It's difficult to go back and start again. It's like mending something you know is bound to break again sooner or later. I am so far removed from all that now. I can't go back to the past. It's not in my nature to be discourteous but I won't ask you to sit down . . . you belong to another man now and you're not the same person I was married to once.

GERDA: Have I changed so much?

THE MAN: Your voice, your eyes, your movements are those of a stranger.

GERDA: Have I aged so much?

THE MAN: I don't know. They say that every atom in your body is renewed every three years and every five years you're a completely new person. So to me you are now a totally different person from the one who used to sit here, bored. I can hardly bring myself to call you by your first name; you're like a stranger. And I expect I'd feel the same about my daughter.

GERDA: Don't talk like that. I'd rather you were angry.

THE MAN: Why should I be angry?

GERDA: After all the terrible things I have done to you.

THE MAN: Have you? I don't recall any.

GERDA: Didn't you see the writ?

THE MAN: No, I passed it on to my solicitor. *(Sits down.)*

GERDA: And the verdict?

THE MAN: I didn't read that either. I have no intention of marrying again so I don't need papers like that. *(Pause. Gerda sits down.)* What was the verdict then? That I was too old for you, sexually? *(Gerda nods in the affirmative.)* Well, it was the truth, so why are you embarrassed? I said the very same thing in my counter-writ and I asked the court to release you from your marriage bond.

GERDA: Did you really ask that?

THE MAN: I didn't put it in writing that I was too old, but I said I was getting too old for *you*.

GERDA: *(Hurt)* For me?

THE MAN: Yes, I couldn't very well say that I was too old for you when we got married because then the arrival of our child might have caused some suspicions, and it was our child after all, wasn't it?

GERDA: You know it is. But . . .

THE MAN: Am I to be condemned because I'm growing old? If I should suddenly decide to dance "The Boston" at my age or play cards all through the night I wouldn't have the stamina any more. I would probably collapse with exhaustion and surely that would be more undignified, don't you think?

GERDA: You don't look your age . . .

THE MAN: Did you think the divorce would finish me? *(Gerda doesn't show what she feels.)* Some people thought you'd be the end of me. Do I look a finished man, do you think? *(Gerda is embarrassed.)* Your friends have drawn caricatures of me and had them published in some papers, I've been told. But I don't want you to have a bad conscience about me.

GERDA: Why did you marry me in the first place?

THE MAN: Surely you know why a man wants to get married? You also know that I didn't exactly have to beg for your love. And don't you remember how we both smiled at all those busy-bodies who advised against our union. But why did you tempt me? I've never understood that. Soon after the wedding you didn't even look at me. And even at the reception you behaved as if you were attending someone else's wedding. I thought you might have conspired with my enemies to kill me. At

work, all my subordinates hated me because I was their
superior but they soon made friends with you. Every
new enemy of mine became a friend of yours. That
caused me to say: One must not hate one's enemies,
true, but you shouldn't love my enemies either.
However, when I became aware of your true nature, I
started to be on my guard. But first I wanted proof
that you had told lies and that is why I waited until the
baby was born.

GERDA: I never knew that you could be so deceitful.

THE MAN: I kept quiet, but I never lied. You gradually turned my
former friends into spies and you lured my brother into
deceiving me as well. But the worst of all was that you
made me doubt the legitimacy of my own child.

GERDA: I've taken it all back!

THE MAN: A word once airborne cannot be recalled. But the worst
thing of all is that this false rumour has now reached
the ears of our daughter and she thinks that her mother
is a . . .

GERDA: Oh, no!

THE MAN: Yes, that is so. You built a whole tower on a
foundation of lies, and now this tower of lies will fall
on top of you.

GERDA: It's not true.

THE MAN: Oh yes, I saw Ann-Charlotte a minute ago.

GERDA: Have you met her?

THE MAN: We met on the stairs and she called me "uncle". Do
you know what an uncle is? It is an old friend of the
family, especially of the wife. I am known as her
"uncle" at her school as well. It's horrible for the child.

GERDA: So you've met her then?

THE MAN: Yes, but I didn't want to talk about it. The meeting
was so upsetting that I erased it from my mind.

GERDA: What can I do to make up for everything?

THE MAN:	There's nothing you can do. It's entirely up to me. *(They regard each other in silence.)* And I've already done something about it.
GERDA:	Everything I do seems to go wrong. Can I ask you to forget and forgive . . .
THE MAN:	What do you mean?
GERDA:	Restore, repair . . .
THE MAN:	Do you mean to tie the knot again? To resume your old role as mistress of my house? No thank you, I don't want you.
GERDA:	I never thought I'd hear you say that.
THE MAN:	I'm sure it does you good.

Short pause.

GERDA:	That's a very pretty table runner.
THE MAN:	Yes, it's pretty.
GERDA:	Where did it come from?

Pause.

Louise appears in the doorway leading to the pantry. She has a bill in her hand.

THE MAN:	*(Turns round.)* Is that a bill? *(Gerda gets up, pulls her gloves on. Some buttons fall off. The Man produces some money to pay the bill.)* Eighteen seventy-two. You can keep the change.
LOUISE:	Can you spare a moment, please?
THE MAN:	*(Gets up, walks towards the door, where Louise whispers something to him.)* Oh, my god . . . *(Louise exits.)* Poor Gerda!
GERDA:	What do you mean? Do you think I'm jealous of your maid.
THE MAN:	No, that's not what I meant.
GERDA:	Yes, you did. And you say you're too old for me. But not for her. I'm deeply offended . . . of course she's beautiful. I don't deny that, for a maid that is . . .

THE MAN: Poor Gerda!

GERDA: Why do you keep on saying that?

THE MAN: Because I feel sorry for you. You . . . jealous of my
            servant. That's enough to redress the balance . . .

GERDA: Me jealous?

THE MAN: Why else should you fly into such a temper about my
            quiet young relative?

GERDA: More than a relative . . .

THE MAN: No, my dear. I have given up that sort of thing a long
            time ago. I'm quite happy on my own. *(Pause)* Mr
            Fischer has apparently left with Mr Starck's eighteen-
            year-old daughter.

GERDA: I knew that he had gone, but I didn't know he'd gone
            with another woman. Are you satisfied now?

THE MAN: No, I'm not satisfied. But it's comforting to know that
            there is some justice in the world at least –
            circumstances change so quickly and now you're in the
            same situation that I was in earlier.

GERDA: Her eighteen years compared to my twenty-nine. I'm
            old . . . too old for him.

THE MAN: Everything is relative. By the way, where is the child?

GERDA: Oh, my child! I had quite forgotten . . . my child! Oh
            God! Help me, please. He has taken our child with
            him. He loved Ann-Charlotte like his own daughter.
            Please come with me to the police. Please come with
            me.

THE MAN: Me? No, you ask too much of me.

GERDA: Help me!

THE MAN: *(Walks towards the door on the right.)* Karl Fredrik, will
            you hail a cab and take Gerda to the police station.
            (Short pause.) Don't you want to?

THE
BROTHER: *(Enters)* Of course I want to. We're only human after
            all.

THE MAN: Quickly then. But don't tell Mr Starck. It can still be put right. I feel sorry for him. And for Gerda . . . But hurry up.

GERDA: *(Looking out of the window.)* It's beginning to rain. Could you lend me an umbrella, do you think? Eighteen . . . she's only eighteen. Hurry up. *(She exits with the Brother.)*

THE MAN: "The peaceful existence of old age". And my child in the hands of an adventurer! Louise! *(Louise enters.)* Come and have game of chess with me, please.

LOUISE: Has the consul . . .?

THE MAN: He's just gone out. Is it still raining?

LOUISE: No, it seems to have stopped.

THE MAN: Then I think I'll go for a walk. I need to cool down a little. *(Pause)* You're a good, sensible girl. Do you know Mr Starck's daughter?

LOUISE: Only by sight.

THE MAN: Is she beautiful?

LOUISE: Yes.

THE MAN: Do you know the people who live above us?

LOUISE: No, I've never seen them.

THE MAN: You're evasive.

LOUISE: I've learnt to be reticent.

THE MAN: I think your aloofness can go too far. Will you please make some tea. I'm just going for a short walk. And one more thing: you have seen what has passed here today but I would appreciate it if you don't ask any questions.

LOUISE: I'm not inquisitive by nature.

THE MAN: Thank you.

SCENE THREE

House front, the same as in Scene One. Mr Starck's basement flat is lit up, so is the flat on the first floor, where the windows are open and the blinds pulled up. Mr Starck is outside his door.

THE MAN: *(Sitting on the green bench.)* Quite a shower we had!

MR STARCK: Yes, a blessed shower – it will help the raspberries.

THE MAN: Can I put an order in for a couple of litres then. I'm afraid we don't make our own jam any more. It just seemed to get mouldy.

MR STARCK: I know. You have to keep a constant watch on them jam jars, like watching little children. Some people believe in adding salicylic acid but I think that's just another of those tricks . . .

THE MAN: Salicylic acid, yes. That's supposed to kill the bacteria . . . that must be a good thing.

MR STARCK: But the trouble is you can't get rid of the taste.

THE MAN: By the way, do you have a telephone?

MR STARCK: No, I don't have a telephone . . .

THE MAN: I see.

MR STARCK: Why do you ask?

THE MAN: I just thought . . . sometimes a telephone comes in handy. Important messages, grocery orders . . .

MR STARCK: Maybe, but sometimes it's good to get away from messages too.

THE MAN: I agree, I agree. I always get palpitations whenever the phone rings. You never know what it has in store for you. And I just want peace and quiet.

MR STARCK: Me too.

THE MAN: *(Looks at his watch.)* Isn't it time they lit the gas lamps?

MR STARCK: Maybe he's forgotten us. The lights are already on along the avenue.

THE MAN: Then he must be here soon. I'm quite looking forward to having this lamp on again. *(The telephone rings,*

Louise appears in the dining-room to answer it. The Man rises, puts his hand to his heart, tries to listen. Pause. Louise joins the two men.) What news?

LOUISE: Nothing has changed.

THE MAN: Was it my brother?

LOUISE: No, it was your . . . wife.

THE MAN: What did she want?

LOUISE: She wanted to talk to you.

THE MAN: I don't want to talk to her. Why should I comfort my executioner? I have done it before but now I'm tired of it. Look up there! They have left their lights on. Empty rooms when they're lit up are more terrifying than dark rooms . . . you become aware of the ghosts. *(In a whisper.)* And what about Agnes, do you think Starck knows anything about it?

LOUISE: It's difficult to tell. He doesn't open his heart to people, nor does anyone else in this silent house for that matter.

THE MAN: Should we tell him, do you think?

LOUISE: For God's sake, no.

THE MAN: But it's not the first time she has given him cause for concern.

LOUISE: He never talks about her . . .

THE MAN: It's terrible. Will it never end? *(The telephone rings inside.)* It's ringing again. Don't go. I don't want to know anything. My child . . . in that company. An adventurer and a slut. It's unbelievable. Poor Gerda!

LOUISE: It's better to tell him. I'll go in. You must say something.

THE MAN: I can't move. I'm no good at attacking, even though I'm used to being attacked.

LOUISE: But whenever you try to avoid some danger you always fall victim to it in the end, and if you don't put up any resistance you'll be knocked down.

THE MAN: But if you don't get involved they can't reach you.

LOUISE: Can't reach you?

THE MAN: It's always much better if you don't get too involved.
            What can I do in the midst of so many passionate
            feelings? I can't cool their passion or steer them away.

LOUISE: But what about the child?

THE MAN: I have renounced all claims . . . and besides, to be
            honest with you, I'm not too concerned, especially not
            after she came here and demolished my beautiful
            memories of the past. She destroyed all the beautiful
            images I had hidden away and now there is nothing
            left.

LOUISE: That must be a relief!

THE MAN: Look, how empty it is in there. As if someone has
            moved out. And up there, it looks burnt out . . .

LOUISE: Who is coming over there? *(Agnes enters, upset. Controls
            herself, goes towards the main door where her father is
            sitting.)* It's Agnes. What do you think that means?

THE MAN: Agnes! Then everything will go back to normal again.

MR STARCK: *(Quite composed.)* Good evening, my child. Where have
            you been?

AGNES: I've just been for a walk.

MR STARCK: Your mother has asked after you several times.

AGNES: Has she? Well, here I am.

MR STARCK: Please go down and give your mum a hand with the
            ovens.

AGNES: Is she cross with me?

MR STARCK: She is never cross with you.

AGNES: Oh yes, she is. But she doesn't say anything.

MR STARCK: Lucky you, then.

            Agnes goes in.

THE MAN: *(To Louise.)* Does he know, or doesn't he?

LOUISE: I hope he doesn't . . .

THE MAN: But what has happened? Have they broken up? *(To Mr Starck.)* Listen, Starck.

MR STARCK: Yes, what?

THE MAN: I just thought . . . did you see anyone leaving this house a short while ago?

MR STARCK: I saw an iceman and a postman, I think.

THE MAN: I see. *(To Louise.)* Maybe we were mistaken. I don't know what to think . . . maybe he's pulling our leg. What did Gerda say when she rang?

LOUISE: She wanted to talk to you.

THE MAN: How did she sound? Was she upset?

LOUISE: Yes.

THE MAN: I'm afraid I find it rather immodest of her to appeal to me under these circumstances.

LOUISE: But what about the child?

THE MAN: Do you know, I met my daughter on the stairs and when I asked her if she recognized me, she called me "uncle". And then she went on to inform me that her father was upstairs. She meant her stepfather. He has the legal rights over her. They have slandered me and made me redundant.

LOUISE: A cab just stopped round the corner.

            Mr Starck goes into his apartment.

THE MAN: I only hope they don't come back. I don't want to be saddled with them all the time . . . having to listen to my child singing her new father's praises, and then we shall be back to the beginning again: "Why did you marry me?" – "You know why, but why did you want to marry me?" – "You know why . . ." and so on until the end of time.

LOUISE: The consul is coming.

THE MAN: How does he look?

LOUISE: He doesn't appear to be in a hurry.

THE MAN: He's probably rehearsing what he's going to say to me. Does he look pleased with himself?

LOUISE: Thoughtful rather than pleased, I'd say.

THE MAN: I see . . . yes, he always was the thoughtful one. But as soon as he got near to that woman he would betray me . . . every time . . . She could charm anyone, except me. To me she appeared coarse, simple, plain and silly, but to others she seemed refined, gracious, beautiful and intelligent. All the resentment that my independence gave rise to turned into sympathy for her instead. And through her they tried to master and influence me, hurt me and finish me in the end.

LOUISE: I'll wait by the telephone. I think it's going to clear up soon.

THE MAN: People don't want you to be independent. They prefer obedience; all my subordinates right down to the caretaker wanted me to obey them. But when I didn't want to obey, they accused me of being a tyrant. Every maid I've ever had has always wanted me to obey her. They served me food which was heated up and when I refused to eat it, they turned my wife against me and in the end my wife wanted me to obey the child. But at that point I left. That's how the conspiracy against the tyrant – me – came about. Off you go now, Louise. We're about to set fire to the mine-field out there. *(The Brother enters from the left.)* Well, what is the upshot then? But spare me the details, please.

THE BROTHER: Let me sit down first. I'm a little tired.

THE MAN: It's been raining. The bench is wet . . .

THE BROTHER: But you're sitting on it. It can't be that bad then, can it?

THE MAN: As you like. Where is my daughter?

THE BROTHER: Let me start from the beginning.

THE MAN: Please.

THE
BROTHER: (*Slowly*) I arrived at the station with Gerda – and at
            the ticket office I saw Agnes and him . . .

THE MAN: So Agnes was with him?

THE
BROTHER: Yes, and so was your daughter. Gerda stayed outside
            while I went up to them. At that moment he handed
            over the tickets to Agnes, but when she saw that they
            were third class tickets she threw them back in his face
            and rushed out to hail a cab.

THE MAN: Oh dear.

THE
BROTHER: And while I was trying to get an explanation from the
            man, Gerda rushed forward and snatched the child
            from his arms and disappeared in the crowd.

THE MAN: What did he say?

THE
BROTHER: You know: "when you hear the other side" etc . . .

THE MAN: I want to know. He can't be as bad as we have
            imagined, of course. He must have his good sides too
            . . .

THE
BROTHER: Yes, exactly.

THE MAN: I understand. But surely you don't expect me to listen
            to you praising my enemy.

THE
BROTHER: No, not praising but there are mitigating circumstances
            . . .

THE MAN: Did you ever want to listen to me when I told you the
            truth about our situation? You listened alright but your
            only answer consisted of a disapproving silence. As if
            you thought I was lying. You have always been on the
            side of wrong-doers and you thought I was lying
            because you were enchanted by Gerda yourself. But
            there was another reason . . .

THE
BROTHER:　Don't carry on, my dear brother. You can only see things from your point of view.

THE MAN:　How do you expect me to see my situation – from the enemy's point of view? Surely I can't be expected to undermine myself?

THE
BROTHER:　I'm not your enemy.

THE MAN:　You are when you befriend the person who has hurt me so much. Where is my child now?

THE
BROTHER:　I don't know.

THE MAN:　How did it all end at the railway station?

THE
BROTHER:　He took a train to the south.

THE MAN:　And the others?

THE
BROTHER:　Vanished.

THE MAN:　That means they could all be back again. *(Pause)* Did you notice if they took the train too?

THE
BROTHER:　No, he left alone.

THE MAN:　Then I'm rid of him anyway. Problem number two remains: mother and child.

THE
BROTHER:　Why are the lights on up there?

THE MAN:　They forgot to switch them off.

THE
BROTHER:　I'll go and do it.

THE MAN:　No, don't go. I only hope they won't come back. Repetition, repetition, forever repetitions.

THE
BROTHER:　But things are looking up at least.

THE MAN:　The worst remains. Do you think they'll come back?

THE
BROTHER: Not her, not after being humiliated like that in Louise's presence.

THE MAN: I had forgotten. She actually did me the honour of being jealous. I believe there might be some justice in the world after all.

THE
BROTHER: And when she heard that Agnes was so much younger . . .

THE MAN: Poor Gerda! But in cases like these it's no good referring to Divine Justice because people don't really want justice. We must treat obscenity gently. And Nemesis – Divine Nemesis is only meant for others. That was the telephone again. It sounds like a rattlesnake. *(Louise can be seen by the telephone. Pause. To Louise.)* Did the snake bite?

LOUISE: *(By the window.)* May I interrupt . . .

THE MAN: Please, let's hear the news . . .

LOUISE: Your wife has gone to see her mother in Dalarna and she intends to stay there . . . with the child.

THE MAN: *(To his brother.)* Mother and child gone to the country, to a good home. A good solution. Oh!

LOUISE: And she asked me to switch the lights off in their flat.

THE MAN: Yes, you'd better do that at once. And pull down the blinds as well, please.

Louise exits.

Mr Starck reappears.

MR STARCK: *(Looking towards the sky.)* I think it's clearing up. The storm has passed.

THE MAN: Yes, the sky seems to have cleared. That means we'll be able to see the moon tonight.

MR STARCK: It was a blessed rain. Wonderful rain.

The Lamp-Lighter enters, lights the gas lamp.

THE MAN: The first gas lamp of the season. Now autumn is here, the season for old men. Dusk may fall earlier from now on, but we've got our reason to light the way instead. *(Louise appears in the upstairs window for a moment. Then it is suddenly dark up there. To Louise.)* Shut the windows and pull down the blinds, please. And we'll leave our memories in peace. The peace of old age . . . *(A long pause.)* This autumn I shall move away from here.

THE END

Opus 2
AFTER THE FIRE

CHARACTERS

THE IRONMONGER	(Rudolf Valström)
THE STRANGER	(His brother, Arvid Valström)
THE BRICKLAYER	(Mr Andersson; brother-in-law to the nurseryman)
OLD WOMAN	(His wife)
NURSERYMAN	(Mr Gustavsson, brother-in-law to the bricklayer)
ALFRED	(His son)
STONE-MASON	(Second cousin to Albert Eriksson, the hearse driver)
MATILDA	(His daughter)
THE HEARSE DRIVER	
PLAIN CLOTHES POLICEMAN	
THE HOUSEPAINTER	(Mr Sjöblom)
MRS VESTERLUND	(Landlady at The Last Nail, once nanny at the ironmonger's)
WIFE	(The ironmonger's wife)
STUDENT	

SCENE ONE

*The left side of the up-stage area is occupied by the remaining walls of
a burnt-down one-storey house; remnants of wallpaper and tiled stoves
can be seen.*

*At the back, a garden with fruit trees in bloom. To the right an inn with
a wreath hanging on a pole. Outside the inn tables and benches. To the
left, in the foreground, some pieces of furniture and household goods that
have been rescued from the fire are heaped in a pile.*

*The Painter is busy painting the window frames of the inn. He listens to
all conversation that is going on around him. The Bricklayer is digging in
the ruins.*

PLAIN
CLOTHES
POLICEMAN : *(Enters)* Has the fire gone out completely now?

BRICKLAYER : I can't see any smouldering, anyway.

POLICEMAN : I've got a few more questions to ask you, if you don't
mind. *(Pause)* You said you were born and bred in this
district?

BRICKLAYER : That's right. Seventy-five years I've lived in this street;
this house was here before I was born even. Me dad
helped to build this house, you know. He was a
bricklayer too . . .

POLICEMAN : So you know the people around here then?

BRICKLAYER : We all know each other 'round here. There's something
special about this street; once you've moved in here you
never get away. I mean . . . those who move away
always come back . . . sooner or later . . . until they're
carted off into the boneyard at the far end of the street,
that is.

POLICEMAN : You have a special name for this neighbourhood?

BRICKLAYER : Yeah, we call it the Swamp; they all hate each other,
they're all suspicious of each other, they slander and
torment each other . . .

           Pause.

POLICEMAN : Listen, the fire broke out at half past ten in the evening; do you know if the entrance to the building was locked then?

BRICKLAYER : I couldn't tell. You see, I live in the house opposite . . .

POLICEMAN : Where did the fire start then?

BRICKLAYER : In the garret room . . . where the student lives.

POLICEMAN : Was he at home at the time of the accident?

BRICKLAYER : No, he was at the theatre.

POLICEMAN : Had he left his lamp burning?

BRICKLAYER : Oh . . . I couldn't tell . . .

POLICEMAN : Is the student related to the proprietor?

BRICKLAYER : No, I don't think so. – Are you from the police?

POLICEMAN : How come the inn didn't catch fire?

BRICKLAYER : They covered it with a tarpaulin and hosed it down.

POLICEMAN : It's odd the apple trees weren't destroyed by the heat.

BRICKLAYER : They were in bud, you see and it had been raining during the day so they burst into bloom in the middle of the night . . . because of the heat, a little prematurely so to speak, because if we get frost now, our nurseryman will be in a sorry pickle.

POLICEMAN : What sort of a man is this . . . nurseryman?

BRICKLAYER : He's called Gustavsson . . .

POLICEMAN : But what sort of a man?

BRICKLAYER : Listen, sir, I'm seventy-five . . . and I've got nothing against Gustavsson; even if I did I wouldn't tell you about it, would I now?

Pause.

POLICEMAN : I've got the houseowner's name down here as Valström, an ironmonger, sixty years of age . . . approximately . . . married . . .

BRICKLAYER : Carry on if you like! I won't answer any more of your questions.

POLICEMAN: Does anyone suspect that this is a case of arson?

BRICKLAYER: As soon as there's a fire people always suspect arson.

POLICEMAN: Who is the suspect then?

BRICKLAYER: Those with vested interests are always suspected by the insurance company; that's why I've never bothered with insurances.

POLICEMAN: Have you unearthed anything while you've been digging?

BRICKLAYER: All the door keys usually turn up because no one has time to remove them when the house is on fire . . . except occasionally, very occasionally . . .

POLICEMAN: There were no electric lights in the house?

BRICKLAYER: Not in this old house. Just as well, if you ask me, because now they can't blame it on a short circuit, anyway.

POLICEMAN: Blame? Just as well! Listen . . .

BRICKLAYER: Trying to catch me out, are you? I wouldn't if I were you, because then I'll take it all back.

POLICEMAN: Take it all back? You can't do that.

BRICKLAYER: Can't I?

POLICEMAN: No.

BRICKLAYER: Yes, I can. There are no witnesses.

POLICEMAN: Aren't there?

BRICKLAYER: No.

Policeman coughs. A witness enters from left.

POLICEMAN: Here is one witness.

BRICKLAYER: You sly fox!

POLICEMAN: I use my common sense even though I'm not seventy-five like you. *(To the witness.)* Come, let's go and have a word with the nurseryman. *(They exit left.)*

BRICKLAYER: Now I'm in a fine state. That's what happens when I can't keep my mouth shut. *(His wife enters with a lunch packet.)* I'm glad you came.

WIFE: Now, let's have something to eat, dear. You must be
                 hungry after all this to-do . . . I wonder if Gustavsson
                 will scrape through . . . he'd already made a start in the
                 green-houses and he was just about to dig up the
                 flower beds . . . go on, eat up . . . look, Sjöblom is at it
                 already with his putty knife . . . it's a miracle that Mrs
                 Vesterlund escaped like she did. Good morning,
                 Sjöblom, you're not short of work now, are you? *(Mrs
                 Vesterlund enters from the inn.)* And good morning to
                 you, Mrs Vesterlund, that was a narrow escape what
                 with one thing and another . . .

MRS
VESTERLUND: I wonder who is going to reimburse me for my loss of
                 earnings. There is a big funeral taking place today . . .
                 and funerals are always my best days, but I had to put
                 away glasses and things . . .

WIFE: Whose funeral is it then, I've seen so many people
                 heading north towards the cemetery and they've
                 stopped here to have a look at the fire too, of course
                 . . .

MRS
VESTERLUND: I don't think it's a proper funeral, I think they're going
                 to raise a tombstone on the bishop's grave or
                 something, but the trouble is the stone-mason's
                 daughter was going to get married to Gustavsson's son,
                 as you know, and he's working in a shop in town, but
                 now the poor man has lost everything. Isn't that his
                 furniture over there?

WIFE: I think some of it belongs to the ironmonger. It was all
                 turfed out in a jiffy. Where's Valström got to then?

MRS
VESTERLUND: He's down at the police station giving evidence.

WIFE: I see, I see. Hmmm . . . Look, who's here then. My
                 cousin with his hearse. Thirsty as always when he
                 comes back . . .

HEARSE
DRIVER: Good morning, Malvina, you've been setting fire to the
                 place, I hear. There's a fine thing . . . wouldn't it be
                 better if they gave you a new house . . . instead of this
                 ramshackle old thing.

MRS
VESTERLUND: God preserve us! Who's had the presence of your
company in the hearse today then?

HEARSE
DRIVER: I can't remember his name now . . . there was only one
carriage and no wreath on the coffin . . .

MRS
VESTERLUND: Not a joy-ride exactly then . . . if you want something
to drink you'll have to go into the kitchen, because I
haven't got sorted out on this side yet, and
Gustavsson's bringing his wreaths here anyway . . .
there's a what'sit in the cemetery today . . .

HEARSE
DRIVER: Yeah, they're going to raise some monument to the
bishop . . . I heard he wrote a lot of books and he used
to collect bugs . . . he was a bug-collector, the old
bugger.

MRS
VESTERLUND: What's that?

HEARSE
DRIVER: He had cork discs that he stuck pins in . . . with flies
on them . . . we don't understand that sort of thing . . .
but I'm sure it's a straight business . . . can I come
into the kitchen now?

MRS
VESTERLUND: Come through the back door then, and I'll give you a
dram . . .

HEARSE
DRIVER: But I want to have a word with Valström before I
leave, I keep my horses here with the stone mason. I
don't think much of him, but we do business together,
that's to say I recommend him when someone dies and
that's why he lets me put my horses in his yard
sometimes. Will you tell me as soon as Valström comes
back . . . lucky he didn't have all his paints here, isn't
it?

*Walks to the back of the inn. Mrs Vesterlund enters
through the door at the front. The Bricklayer has
finished eating, starts digging again.*

WIFE: Did you find anything?

BRICKLAYER: Yes, I found nails and hinges, and all the keys hanging there on the doorpost . . .

WIFE: Were they there when you came or did you put them there?

BRICKLAYER: They've been there all the time.

WIFE: That's funny, that means someone must have closed all the doors and taken the keys out before the fire started. That's strange!

BRICKLAYER: It's a little bit odd, I agree, because it made it harder to put the fire out and save the furniture. Ah, well. Ah, well.

          Pause.

WIFE: I used to work for the Valströms forty years ago, I know the family well, both the ironmonger and his brother who went to America, but I've heard that he's come back; the father was a good sort but the boys . . . rather so-so. Mrs Vesterlund looked after that Rudolf, they never got on, you know, those brothers, always fighting and squabbling. I've seen a thing or two . . . A lot of things have passed in this house, probably about time it was smoked out. Oh dear, what a house. They came and went, one after the other . . . but they all came back here to die in the end . . . they were born here, they got married here and they were divorced here. And the brother Arvid, the one that went to America, was thought to be dead for many years . . . anyway . . . he didn't claim his inheritance, but now they say he's back again . . . but no one has seen him, of course . . . there's so much talk. Look, here is Valström back from the police station.

BRICKLAYER: He doesn't look too happy, but I suppose that's understandable under the circumstances . . . But who was that student who rented the room in the attic? They all stick together around here.

WIFE: Oh . . . I don't know. He joined the family for meals . . . I think he gave some private lessons to the children.

BRICKLAYER: And to the mistress of the house?

WIFE: No, they played whatever it's called . . . tennis . . . and
                   they squabbled too. Everyone seems to be squabbling
                   and running each other down around here . . .

BRICKLAYER: Yes, when they broke into the student's room they
                   found lots of hairpins on the floor, it's all brought to
                   light in the end but not until it's been through the fire
                   . . .

WIFE: I don't think it was Valström, you know, but his
                   brother-in-law, that Gustavsson . . .

BRICKLAYER: He's always in a temper but today he's worse than ever
                   . . . and now I suppose he'll demand his money from
                   me as well since he's lost out on the fire . . .

WIFE: Shhh!

NURSERY-
MAN: *(Enters with funeral wreaths etc.)* I wonder if I'll sell
                   anything today. If I don't, we won't have any money
                   for food after this spectacle.

BRICKLAYER: Weren't you insured then?

NURSERY-
MAN: Yes, I'd insured the glass in the green-houses, but this
                   year I was trying to be economical so I just had oiled
                   paper. How could I be such a fool? *(Scratches his head.)*
                   And they won't pay for that. Six hundred paper
                   windows I'll have to cut out and glue together and treat
                   with oil again. Well, they always said that I was the
                   stupidest of us seven brothers and sisters, what an ass,
                   what a block-head I've been. And then I went drinking
                   last night too. Why the dickens did I have to go
                   drinking yesterday of all days? Just when I could do
                   with some brains today. It was the stone-mason who
                   invited me for a drink. You see, our children are
                   getting married tonight, but I should have said no all
                   the same. I didn't want to. But I'm a shit who can't say
                   no. And it's the same when it comes to lending money.
                   I can't say no. It's really too bad. And then that
                   'copper' came and asked me all sorts of questions,

trying to trap me, no doubt. I should have shut up like the painter over there, but I can't keep my mouth shut, so I told him this and that and he wrote it all down and now they've called me to testify.

BRICKLAYER: What did you tell him?

NURSERY-
MAN: I said I thought it seemed an insane thing to do . . . setting fire to the whole house.

BRICKLAYER: Did you say that?

NURSERY-
MAN: Yeah. Go on, give me what for. I've deserved it. I'm such a fool.

BRICKLAYER: Who do you think set fire to the house then? Don't mind the ironmonger . . . and my wife won't run with any gossip.

NURSERY-
MAN: Who set fire to it? Why, the student of course. It started in his room in the attic.

BRICKLAYER: No, it didn't. It started under his study!

NURSERY-
MAN: Oh, did it? What have I done . . . I'll come to a bad end. Under his study? What was under his study then? The kitchen?

BRICKLAYER: No, there was a wardrobe. See for yourself. The cook's wardrobe.

NURSERY-
MAN: Then she must have done it.

BRICKLAYER: But don't say that before you know for sure.

NURSERY-
MAN: The stone-mason wasn't very nice to the cook yesterday. He knew a thing or two, I wouldn't be surprised . . .

WIFE: You shouldn't repeat what he said because you can never trust a person who's been inside . . .

NURSERY-
MAN: That was a long time ago . . . anyway the cook was a

dragon and she was always haggling over the price of vegetables . . .

WIFE: Here's our ironmonger . . . straight from the police station . . . Shhh! *(The Stranger enters, wearing a frock-coat, top hat with a piece of crape and a walking stick.)* It's not the ironmonger, but he looks just like him!

STRANGER: How much is this wreath?

NURSERY-
MAN: Fifty *ore*.

STRANGER: That's not expensive.

NURSERY-
MAN: Well, I'm such an ass I can't charge the going rate.

STRANGER: *(Looking around.)* Has there been a fire here?

NURSERY-
MAN: Yes, there was a fire here last night.

STRANGER: Oh, my God. *(Pause)* Whose house?

NURSERY-
MAN: Mr Valström's.

STRANGER: The ironmonger's?

NURSERY-
MAN: Yes, the ironmonger's.

   Pause.

STRANGER: Where is he?

NURSERY-
MAN: I expect he'll be here in a minute.

STRANGER: Then I'll go for a walk first. I'll leave the wreath here in the meantime. I'm going to the cemetery later, you see.

NURSERY-
MAN: Are you going to see the bishop's monument?

STRANGER: Which bishop?

NURSERY-
MAN: Bishop Stecksén in the Swedish Academy, of course.

STRANGER: Is he dead?

NURSERY-
MAN: Yes, he died a long time ago.

STRANGER: I see. I'll leave the wreath here for the time being.

                Exits left, looking carefully at the ruins.

WIFE: Do you think he was from the insurance company?

BRICKLAYER: No, not that one, then he would have asked quite
                different questions.

WIFE: But he looked very much like the ironmonger.

BRICKLAYER: He was taller than him.

NURSERY-
MAN: I just remembered . . . I need a bouquet for the
                wedding tonight, my son's getting married and I
                haven't got any flowers and my black coat's lost in the
                fire. Damn . . . Madam Vesterlund was going to give
                me some myrtle for the bridal crown, she's the bride's
                godmother. She'd taken some myrtle cuttings from the
                ironmonger's cook, which she'd got from his first wife,
                the one who ran away, you know, but I was going to
                make a nice wreath of it and I quite forgot. I'm the
                biggest fool that ever walked this earth. *(Opens the door
                to the inn.)* Mrs Vesterlund, can I have the myrtle now
                so I can get it finished. I said, can I have the myrtle
                now? – A wreath as well? Will there be enough for that
                too? – No, I didn't think so. – Then I'll forget the
                wedding, that's all. – They'll have to go to the vicar
                and ask him to solemnize their vows, and leave it at
                that but the stone-mason will go mad. – What shall I
                do then? – I can't, – I haven't slept a wink all night. –
                This is too much for an ordinary mortal. – Yes, I'm a
                wretched soul, I know, you just lay in to me. – Here's
                the pot, thank you, and a pair of scissors too, please.
                No I haven't got any, and some wire and string as well;
                where shall I get that from? – I don't know anyone
                who wants to leave their work to run an errand. – I'm
                fed up with the whole thing . . . when you've struggled
                for fifty years and then everything vanishes in a fire
                . . . I'm too old to start all over again, and it all
                happens at the same time, one thing after another. You
                know, I think I'll just get away from it all . . . *(Exits)*

IRON-
MONGER: *(Enters, shaken, badly dressed, his hands are coloured black and blue.)* Is the fire completely out now, Andersson?

BRICKLAYER: Yes, now it's out.

IRON-
MONGER: Have you unearthed anything?

BRICKLAYER: You bet! What the snow covers, the thaw discovers.

IRON-
MONGER: What do you mean, Andersson?

BRICKLAYER: I mean, if you go on digging, you'll find something.

IRON-
MONGER: Have you found something which could explain how the fire started?

BRICKLAYER: No, that's not what I meant.

IRON-
MONGER: Then we're all still under suspicion, all of us.

BRICKLAYER: Surely not me.

IRON-
MONGER: Oh yes, you've been seen in the attic at an unusual hour.

BRICKLAYER: I can't always go looking for my tools at usual hours. When I repaired that stove in the student's room, I left my hammer behind.

IRON-
MONGER: And the stone-mason, the nurseryman, Madam Vesterlund, even the painter . . . we're all under suspicion, the student and the cook and me most of all. It was lucky I paid my insurance premium the day before, otherwise I would have come to a bad end. Just think . . . the stone-mason suspected of arson! Him of all people. He's so afraid of putting a foot wrong nowadays. He's so conscientious that if you ask him what the time is he'll tell you he can't swear on it because his clock may be fast . . . or slow. We all know about the two years he spent inside, he righted himself and now I bet he's the most honest person in the neighbourhood.

BRICKLAYER: But the court will suspect him because he erred once
and his reputation has suffered as a consequence.

IRON-
MONGER: Yes, there are ways and ways of looking at things. Yes.
But you'd better go now . . . you're off to a wedding
tonight, aren't you?

BRICKLAYER: Yes, the wedding, that's right . . . Oh, someone was
looking for you this morning, by the way. He said he'd
be back soon.

IRON-
MONGER: Who was it?

BRICKLAYER: He didn't say.

IRON-
MONGER: Was he a policeman?

BRICKLAYER: No, I don't think so. There he is. *(Exits with his wife.)*

*The Stranger enters. The Ironmonger regards him first
with curiosity then with horror. Wants to run away,
but can't.*

IRON-
MONGER: Arvid!

STRANGER: Rudolf!

IRON-
MONGER: Is it you?

STRANGER: Yes.

IRON-
MONGER: I thought you were dead.

STRANGER: Well, in a way, I suppose I am. I've come from
America . . . after thirty years something pulled, I had
to see my childhood home again, but what do I find
. . . ruins. *(Pause)* It burnt down last night?

IRON-
MONGER: Yes, you came just in time. *(Pause)*

STRANGER: *(Slowly)* That's where it used to be. Such a small space
when you think that it was the home of so many
destinies. There's the dining-room with the painted

walls, palms, cypresses, temples beneath a rosy sky. I
used to dream that that's how the world looked once
you got away from home. And the stove with the faint
flowers which grew out of shells . . . the niche with the
zinc shutters. I remember when we were children and
moved in here, there was a name engraved in the zinc
then, and grandma told us that a man by that name had
committed suicide in that room. I soon forgot, but later on
in life when I was married to that person's niece I used to
think that my destiny was engraved in this piece of metal.
You don't believe in things like that, do you? But you know
how my marriage ended.

IRON-
MONGER: Yes, I've heard . . .

STRANGER: There's the nursery . . . yes.

IRON-
MONGER: Don't let's go digging among the ruins.

STRANGER: Why not? You can read things in the ashes. That's
           what we used to do as children.

IRON-
MONGER: Why don't you sit down here at the table.

STRANGER: What's this? The eating place 'The Last Nail' . . .
           where the hearse drivers used to stop and where the
           criminals used to be given their last drink before they
           went to the gallows. Who's in charge here now?

IRON-
MONGER: Mrs Vesterlund, my old nurse.

STRANGER: Madam Vesterlund . . . I remember her . . . It's as if
           the bench collapsed under me and I fell back through
           the ages, sixty years into my childhood . . . I can smell
           the nursery, and the pressure on my chest. You always
           used to push me down, because you were bigger than
           me and you were so noisy . . . you scared me. I used to
           hide in the garden because I was frightened. And I was
           pulled out and given a good hiding, always a good
           hiding but I never understood why and I still don't.
           She was my mother after all.

IRON-
MONGER: Shhh.

STRANGER: Yes, you were the favourite and they always liked you
. . . and then we got a stepmother. Her father carted
corpses and we had seen him go past here with his
hearse for years. In the end he grinned and nodded at
us as if he wanted to say "I'll come and take you one
day." And then he did turn up one day and we called
him grandpa. That's when dad married his daughter.

IRON-
MONGER: Nothing sinister about that.

STRANGER: No, but the way it's all woven together, our destinies
and those of others . . .

IRON-
MONGER: It's like that everywhere . . .

STRANGER: Yes, it's all the same, everywhere. When one's young
one sees the loom being set up: the parents, relatives,
friends, acquaintances, servants . . . make up the warp.
Later on in life one can see the weft; and the shuttle of
destiny works the thread forward and back; sometimes
it breaks but it can be tied together again and so it
continues, the beams beat, the wool is forced into
curlicues and then the tapestry is finished. In old age,
when your eye sees, you realise that those funny figures
make up a pattern, a code, an ornament, a hieroglyph
which can only be interpreted when it's finished: this is
life. The world weaver has woven it. *(Pause. He gets
up.)* Is that our family album over there among all the
rubbish? The book of our fates and fortunes.
Grandparents, father and mother, brothers and sisters,
relations, the so-called friends, school-mates, maids,
godparents . . . It's funny, I've been to America,
Australia, Congo and Hongkong, and wherever I've
been I've always come across at least one compatriot.
After exchanging a few words, it soon transpired that
he knew my family or at least a godparent or a maid, or
else we had some acquaintance in common. On the
island of Formosa, I even bumped into a relation . . .

IRON-
MONGER: When did you start to think like this?

STRANGER: I don't know but however my life turned out – and
I've been both rich and poor, high and low . . . I've

been in a shipwreck and an earthquake . . . whatever happened in my life, I always saw a connection and – a repetition. In any one particular situation I saw the result of a previous event. Whenever I met someone I was reminded of someone else from the past. There are also scenes from my life which recur several times and I have frequently said to myself: I've experienced this before. And there have been events which seemed inevitable, or predictable.

IRON-
MONGER: Where have you been all these years?

STRANGER: Everywhere. I've seen life from every perspective . . . from above and below but it's always seemed as if it was staged for me especially, and I've finally reconciled myself with part of my past at least. I've also forgiven my own and other people's so-called faults. You and I, for instance . . . there were a lot of unsettled matters between us. *(Ironmonger looks afraid.)* Don't look so frightened.

IRON-
MONGER: I'm never frightened.

STRANGER: You don't change.

IRON-
MONGER: Nor do you.

STRANGER: Don't you think so? That's interesting. You always consider yourself so brave and I remember when you got that false idea of yourself. You'd jumped head first in the swimming pool and mother said: "Rudolf has real courage!" Meant for me who'd been robbed of all courage and self-confidence. But then one day you stole some apples and you were cowardly enough not to admit it but blamed it on me instead.

IRON-
MONGER: Haven't you forgotten that yet?

STRANGER: I haven't forgotten, but I've forgiven. I can see the apple tree from here . . . that's why I remember it so well. It's over there . . . it's a Jonathan Pippin. And if you look carefully you'll see the marks from a large sawn-off branch. If you remember, I didn't get angry

with you despite that unfair punishment but I was
angry with the tree and I cursed it. Two years later the
large branch dried out and was sawn off. It reminded
me of the fig tree which our Lord cursed once but I
didn't pursue the simile. I still know the names of all
the fruit trees by heart; and once on Jamaica when I
was ill with yellow fever I recited them all. Most of
them are still here, I see. Over there is the Newton
Wonder with its red striated fruit . . . a chaffinch once
built a nest in it . . . over there are the Coxes, just
outside our attic window, where I swotted for my
engineering exam. That one is an Ellison's Orange, and
that one an Eġremont Russet; the Comice pear tree
which looks like a pyramid poplar, and those were the
stewing pears that never ripened . . . which we detested
but mother valued most. A wryneck lived in that old
tree . . . she used to twist her head and shriek horribly
. . . that's fifty years ago now.

IRON-
MONGER: *(Angrily)* What are you trying to say?

STRANGER: As suspicious and foul-tempered as ever. Interesting. –
I have no ulterior motive, the memories just surface
. . . I remember the garden was leased out once, but we
were allowed to walk in it. To me that was like being
expelled from paradise . . . and the Tempter stood
behind every tree. In the autumn when the apples lay
ripe on the ground I fell for the temptation . . . it was
irresistible . . .

IRON-
MONGER: You stole as well?

STRANGER: Of course. But I didn't blame anyone else, especially
not you. Later, when I was about forty, I leased an
orange plantation in the American South . . . well . . .
and I had thieves there every night. I couldn't sleep, I
lost weight, I became ill . . . Then I thought of poor
Gustavsson with his nursery – back here!

IRON-
MONGER: He is still alive!

STRANGER: Maybe he too stole apples in his childhood.

IRON-
MONGER: It's possible.

STRANGER: Why are your hands so black?

IRON-
MONGER: Because I handle dyes . . . or are you referring to
            something else?

STRANGER: What should that be?

IRON-
MONGER: That my hands aren't clean.

STRANGER: Oh!

IRON-
MONGER: Maybe you're thinking of the inheritance.

STRANGER: As small-minded as ever. Just like when you were
            eight.

IRON-
MONGER: And you as carefree, philosophical and silly as ever.

STRANGER: Strange . . . How many times have we said that to each
            other? *(Pause)* I'm looking at your album here . . . at
            our brothers and sisters. Five of them dead now.

IRON-
MONGER: Yes.

STRANGER: And our school-friends?

IRON-
MONGER: "Some have been taken and some have been left".

STRANGER: I came across one of them once in South Carolina . . .
            Axel Eriksson, do you remember him?

IRON-
MONGER: Of course.

STRANGER: During one long night that we spent together on a train
            he told me that our respected family – which enjoyed
            such a good reputation, was in fact full of villains and
            they made their fortune mostly through smuggling
            goods and that this house was built with walls of
            double thickness so they could hide their goods. Can
            you see that there are double walls?

IRON-
MONGER: *(Crushed)* That's why we had so many wardrobes
            everywhere.

STRANGER: Eriksson's father had been working at the customs, he
            knew our father and he told me things that turned my
            whole world upside down.

IRON-
MONGER: Why didn't you hit him then?

STRANGER: Why should I do that? But my hairs turned grey that
            night and I had to review my whole life. You know, we
            lived in mutual admiration and we thought our family
            was the best one possible, we almost worshipped our
            parents. But now I had to remodel their faces, undress
            them, pull them down and banish them from my mind.
            It was terrible. And then they popped up again as
            ghosts; pieces of the jigsaw puzzle were joined, but
            didn't fit and the result was a wax cabinet of monsters.
            All these grey-haired men who kept coming to our
            house . . . whom we bowed to and shook hands with,
            figures playing cards and eating supper . . . they were
            smugglers and some of them had even been in prison.
            Did you know that?

IRON-
MONGER: *(Annihilated)* No.

STRANGER: The whole hardware store was just a hiding-place for
            smuggled knitting wool which was then dyed to make it
            unrecognizable – I remember how I always hated the
            smell of that dye-bath, a disgustingly sweet smell.

IRON-
MONGER: Why did you have to tell me all this?

STRANGER: Why should I keep quiet about it? I don't want you to
            sound ridiculous when you boast about our respectable
            parents. Have you never noticed how people make faces
            behind your back?

IRON-
MONGER: No.

            Pause.

STRANGER: I can see father's book-case among the rubble. Do you
            remember how he always kept it locked. But once when
            he was away I found the key. I'd already noticed the
            books at the front – through the glass – they were
            sermons, works by great poets, books on gardening,
            collections of statutes for customs and excise, books on
            law, and one about foreign coins and one book on
            technology which was to determine my career, but I
            discovered that behind these books there was space for
            others, and I explored a little; first I found the cane –
            now I know that the bitter plant rattan bears a fruit
            from which we can extract the red colouring called
            Dragon's blood, funny isn't it? Beside it, there was a
            jar labelled Arsenic . . .

IRON-
MONGER: Probably to be used for the dyeing.

STRANGER: In more ways than one, yes. But now to the point:
            there were piles of booklets with illustrated covers
            which aroused my interest . . . without going into detail
            . . . they were the memoirs of a certain cavalier. I took
            them out, closed the cupboard and underneath that
            large oak tree over there I studied the book. We call it
            the tree of knowledge, right. And that's how I stepped
            out of the paradise of childhood and was initiated,
            prematurely, into the secrets which . . . well . . .

IRON-
MONGER: You too?

STRANGER: You as well? *(Pause)* Let's talk about something else; all
            that is dead and buried now. Were you insured?

IRON-
MONGER: *(Angry)* You've just asked me that.

STRANGER: Sorry, I forgot. I often mix up what I have said with
            what I intended to say, because I think so intensely,
            ever since the day when I hanged myself in the
            wardrobe.

IRON-
MONGER: What?

STRANGER: I hanged myself in the wardrobe.

IRON-
MONGER: *(Slowly)* Was that what happened that Maundy
Thursday which we were never told about? You were
rushed to hospital?

STRANGER: *(Slowly)* Yes. You see, that's how little we know about
our nearest, our home, our own life.

IRON-
MONGER: But why did you do that?

STRANGER: I was twelve years old and fed up with life. It was like
going into a vast darkness . . . I didn't know why I was
here . . . and I thought the world was a madhouse. I
realised that one day when the whole school was sent
out with torches and banners to celebrate "the destroyer
of our country". I had just read a book which described
our country's worst monarch as the country's destroyer
and here we were – celebrating this man with hymns
and praises.

       Pause.

IRON-
MONGER: What happened in hospital?

STRANGER: I ended up in the mortuary, my dear fellow, passed for
dead. I don't know whether I really was, but when I
woke up I had forgotten most of my previous life and I
started afresh but in such a way that all of you thought
I'd become weird. – Have you got married again?

IRON-
MONGER: I have a wife and children. Somewhere.

STRANGER: When I regained consciousness I thought I was
someone else. I faced life with a cynical calm. That's
how it should be, and the worse it got, the more
interesting it was too . . . I regarded myself as another
person and I observed, studied this other man and his
destiny and that made me insensitive to my own
sufferings. But in 'death' I had acquired new skills . . .
I could see right through people, read their thoughts,
hear their opinions. When I was with people I could
visualize them naked . . . where did the fire start?

IRON-
MONGER: Nobody knows.

STRANGER: But I read in the paper that it began in a wardrobe underneath the student's attic room. What's his subject by the way?

IRON-
MONGER: *(Looks frightened.)* Is that what the paper said? I haven't read today's paper yet. What more did it say?

STRANGER: Everything.

IRON-
MONGER: Everything?

STRANGER: It mentioned the double walls, the respectable family of smugglers, the prison sentence, the hairpins . . .

IRON-
MONGER: Which hairpins?

STRANGER: I don't know, but that's what the paper said. Don't you know?

IRON-
MONGER: No.

STRANGER: Everything was revealed and now we can expect a huge crowd to come and look at our misery.

IRON-
MONGER: Good Lord. And you seem to think it's amusing that our family is scandalized?

STRANGER: My family! I've never felt related to you. I've never had any feelings of compassion for my neighbour or myself for that matter. I just find it interesting to watch . . . what sort of a woman is your wife?

IRON-
MONGER: Was there something about her too?

STRANGER: About her and the student, yes.

IRON-
MONGER: Good. Then I was right. You'll see. Just wait and see. – Here comes the stone-mason.

STRANGER: You know him?

IRON-
MONGER: So do you. A school-friend . . . Albert Eriksson.

STRANGER: Whose father used to work in the customs and whose
               brother I met on the train . . . he who was so well
               informed about our family.

IRON-
MONGER: Then it's that bastard who has told the paper.

               Stone-mason enters with a pickaxe. Looks at the ruins.

STRANGER: It was a terrible thing . . .

IRON-
MONGER: He's been inside too, for two years . . . Do you know
               what he did? He erased something from a contract I
               had with a . . .

STRANGER: And you got him locked up . . . and now he has taken
               his revenge.

IRON-
MONGER: The funny thing is that nowadays he is considered the
               most honest fellow in the whole neighbourhood. He has
               become a martyr . . . almost a saint so we hardly dare
               touch him.

STRANGER: Very interesting.

POLICEMAN: *(To the Stone-mason.)* Would you mind pulling down
               this wall?.

STONE-
MASON: The one by the wardrobe, you mean?

POLICEMAN: That's the one, yes.

STONE-
MASON: That's where the fire started and I'm sure we'll find a
               candle or a lamp in there. I know people's habits.

POLICEMAN: Carry on.

STONE-
MASON: The door to the wardrobe was burnt down but the
               floor collapsed so we couldn't discover the cause at the
               time, but now we'll pull the sting out. *(Chips away with
               his pickaxe.)* Here we go! Here we go! Hey-ho, heave-
               ho. Can you see anything?

POLICEMAN: Not yet.

STONE-
MASON: *(As before.)* I can. The lamp's exploded, but the stand is still here. Who recognizes this forfeit? I thought I saw the ironmonger here just now.

POLICEMAN: Yes, he is over there. *(Takes the lamp stand and shows it to him.)* Do you recognize this lamp?

IRON-
MONGER: It's not mine, it belongs to the tutor.

POLICEMAN: The student? Where is he?

IRON-
MONGER: He's in town but he'll probably be back soon because his books are over there.

POLICEMAN: How did his lamp come to end up in the cook's wardrobe? Did he have a relationship with her?

IRON-
MONGER: Probably.

POLICEMAN: As long as he admits that the lamp belongs to him we can arrest him. What do you make of it, sir?

IRON-
MONGER: Me? What can I say?

POLICEMAN: What would be his motive to set fire to another person's property?

IRON-
MONGER: I don't know. Malice, evil, people are so unpredictable. Maybe he wanted to conceal something . . .

POLICEMAN: Not a good idea, because it brings all these nasty things to light. Did he bear a grudge against you?

IRON-
MONGER: Probably. Because I helped him once when he was in trouble and after that he hated me, of course.

POLICEMAN: Of course. *(Pause)* Who is the student then?

IRON-
MONGER: He was brought up in an orphanage, parents unknown.

POLICEMAN: Do you have a grown-up daughter, sir?

IRON-
MONGER: *(Angry)* Of course I have.

POLICEMAN: I see. *(Pause. To the Stone-mason.)* Get your twelve men together now and pull the walls down quickly so we can see what's hidden underneath. *(Exits)*

STONE-
MASON: It won't take a minute. *(Exits)*

Pause.

STRANGER: Did you really pay your insurance premium?

IRON-
MONGER: Of course.

STRANGER: Personally?

IRON-
MONGER: No, I sent someone else, as usual.

STRANGER: You sent someone else. How like you. Shall we take a walk in the garden and have a look at the apple trees?

IRON-
MONGER: Not a bad idea.

STRANGER: We're getting to the interesting bit now.

IRON-
MONGER: Maybe not so interesting, if you get involved.

STRANGER: Me?

IRON-
MONGER: Who knows?

STRANGER: What a complex tapestry.

IRON-
MONGER: You had an illegitimate child at an orphanage, didn't you?

STRANGER: God bless . . . let's take a walk in the garden.

SCENE TWO

*Same set, but the walls are now pulled down so we can see the garden
which is in full bloom with spring flowers: Mezereon, Deutzia, Daffodils,
Narcissi, Tulips, Mountain Cowslips etc. All the fruit trees are in bloom
too.*

*The Stone-mason, the Bricklayer and his Wife, the Nurseryman, the
Hearse Driver, Mrs Vesterlund, the Housepainter stand in a row and look
at the burnt site.*

STRANGER: *(Enters)* There they stand gloating over the disaster,
waiting for the victim which seems to be the main
thing. They regard it as a fact that it must be a case of
arson, because that is what they wish it to be. And all
these crooks are friends from my youth, companions
. . . I'm related to the hearse-driver through my
stepmother whose father carried corpses for a living . . .
(To those present.) Don't stand there, my friends . . .
there could be dynamite in the cellar and we might
have an explosion any minute. *(The crowd disperses.
Stranger at the rubbish heap, looking through books.)*
These books belong to the student. The same rubbish
as in my youth. Livy, Roman history . . . which is
supposed to be a pack of lies, but here is a book from
my brother's collection. 'Columbus or the man who
discovered America'. That's my book . . . which I got
for Christmas in 1857, the name is rubbed out,
someone stole it from me . . . and I accused one of the
maids who was subsequently dismissed. A fine thing,
maybe that was her downfall. Fifty years ago . . . There
is the frame for the family portrait; my splendid
grandfather, the smuggler . . . who was in chains. Fine
thing! But what's this? The bedstead belonging to the
mahogany bed . . . the bed where I was born! Damn.
Item: The legs of a dining table . . . an heirloom . . .
yes, we were told it was of solid ebony, we admired it
and now fifty years later it's proved to be of stained
maple. Everything in our home was stained, to make it
unrecognizable . . . and our clothes were dyed when we
were children, so we were always walking around with
our bodies stained from the dye. Bluff . . . ebony. Here

is the big clock . . . also contraband goods . . . which measured out the time for two generations, was wound up every Saturday when we were given dried cod and a small beer for dinner . . . like a clever clock it used to stop every time someone died. Let me have a look at you. Let's see how you look inside, old friend. *(The clock breaks at the touch.)* Breaks at the touch. That's how it was with everything. Vain, futile. Here is the globe which used to be at the top, but it should have been underneath. You little earth, the densest of all the planets and the heaviest, making it so hard for you to breathe, hard to carry your burden; the cross is your symbol, but it could equally well have been a fool's cap or a strait-jacket . . . the world of illusions and madmen. Oh Eternal One, has your earth got lost in space? And how did it come to spin so fast that your children got giddy and lost their senses . . . so they couldn't see the real thing but only that which appeared real. Amen. Here is the student. *(Student enters. Is looking for someone.)* He is looking for the mistress of the house. And his eyes reveal everything. Happy youth! Who are you looking for?

STUDENT: *(Shy)* I was looking for . . .

STRANGER: Speak up, young man, or keep quiet. I understand you perfectly well.

STUDENT: With whom do I have the honour of . . .

STRANGER: It's no honour speaking to me, you know that. I once ran away to America because I was in debt . . .

STUDENT: That wasn't the right thing to do . . .

STRANGER: Right or wrong, but it's a fact. So you were looking for the mistress of the house . . . she is not here, but she'll probably be here soon, like everyone else, they are all drawn to the fire like mosquitoes . . .

STUDENT: . . . to the light.

STRANGER: You said it . . . I was going to say the lamp, to choose a more apt expression. However, conceal your feelings, young man, if you can, I conceal mine. We were talking about the lamp, yes. What's the story about the lamp?

STUDENT: Which lamp?

STRANGER: What did I say? You're all the same . . . denying everything and full of lies. The lamp in the cook's wardrobe, the one that caused the fire.

STUDENT: I know nothing about that.

STRANGER: Some people blush when they tell lies, others get a white nose. You must have invented a new method.

STUDENT: Are you talking to yourself, sir?

STRANGER: It's a bad habit of mine. Are your parents still alive?

STUDENT: No, they're not.

STRANGER: Now you're lying again, but you don't know it.

STUDENT: I never lie.

STRANGER: Only three times in this short while. I know your father, young man.

STUDENT: I don't believe you.

STRANGER: So much the better . . . for me. See this tie-pin? Beautiful, isn't it? But I never see it myself, I don't get the pleasure of seeing it but other people enjoy looking at it. At least it's not egotistical, and there are moments when I would like to see it on someone else's cravat just so that I can admire it. Do you want it?

STUDENT: I don't understand . . . maybe it's better not to have it, as you said.

STRANGER: Maybe. Don't be so impatient, she'll soon be here. Isn't it wonderful to be your age?

STUDENT: No, I don't think so.

STRANGER: You're not your own master, you eat other people's bread, you're always out of money, not supposed to speak in company, you get treated like a blockhead, and as you can't afford to get married, you cast your eyes on other people's wives with all its dangerous consequences. Hypocritical youth!

STUDENT: Yes, it's true. When you're young you only wish you were grown-up, that's fifteen . . . when you're confirmed and get your top hat; then you wish you were old . . . that's twenty-one. So no one wants to be young, you see.

STRANGER: And when you're really old, you wish you were dead. There's not so much left to wish for then. Do you know that you're about to be arrested?

STUDENT: Me?

STRANGER: Yes, the police told me a minute ago.

STUDENT: Me?

STRANGER: Does that surprise you? Didn't you know that we must be prepared for everything in life?

STUDENT: But what have I done?

STRANGER: You don't need to have done anything to be arrested. It's enough to be suspected of something.

STUDENT: But then anyone could be arrested?

STRANGER: Quite true. If you want things to be just and fair you might as well put a noose around the neck of the whole human species, but one doesn't, that's the trouble. It's a terrible species . . . ugly, sweaty, stinking; unclean linen, dirty socks with holes in them, bunions, corns, ugh! No, an apple tree in bloom is much more beautiful . . . look at the lilies on the ground . . . it's as if they didn't belong here. Have you noticed their scent?

STUDENT: Are you a philosopher, sir?

STRANGER: Yes, I'm a great philosopher.

STUDENT: You're just joking with me.

STRANGER: That's your excuse – so you can get away. Go away then. Hurry up.

STUDENT: I was expecting someone.

STRANGER: I thought so. But I think you'd better go and see her.

STUDENT: Has she told you?

STRANGER: She didn't have to.

STUDENT: I don't want to disappoint her . . . if that is so. *(Exits)*

STRANGER: Is that my son? I too was young once, and that was
neither extraordinary nor amusing. And I'm his . . .
what more? Besides . . . who knows? I'll pay a visit to
Mrs Vesterlund . . . she used to work for my parents,
she was loyal and good-tempered and when she'd been
stealing for ten years, she received an award for faithful
services. *(Sits down at the table.)* Here are Gustavsson's
wreaths, made of bear-berry leaves . . . which he claims to
be cranberry . . . as carelessly bound as forty years ago . . .
everything he did was slipshod or stupid and that's why
things went badly for him. He can be excused a lot because
of his self-awareness, though. "Silly old me", he used to
say and then he took off his cap and scratched his head.
This is a myrtle . . . *(He taps the pot.)* it hasn't been
watered, of course . . . he always forgot to water the plants,
the fool . . . how did he expect them to grow! *(The Painter
becomes visible.)* What sort of a painter is he? Does he
belong to this 'swamp' too? Maybe he has woven a thread
in my tapestry as well? *(The Painter stares at the Stranger.
Stranger stares back.)* Do you recognize me?

HOUSE-
PAINTER: Is it Arvid?

STRANGER: Has been, and is, if to be is to be perceived.

          Pause.

HOUSE-
PAINTER: I ought to be angry with you, really.

STRANGER: Go ahead. But let me know the reason first. So we can
sort it out.

HOUSE-
PAINTER: Do you remember. . . .

STRANGER: Unfortunately I have a very good memory.

HOUSE-
PAINTER: Do you remember a boy called Robert?

STRANGER: Oh yes, he was a real scoundrel, but he was good at
drawing.

HOUSE-
PAINTER: *(Slowly)* And he wanted to get into the Academy
because he wanted to become a painter, an artist. But

that was when colour blindness was in fashion. You, sir, were an engineer in those days and you were asked to examine my eyes before the master, your father, would pay for my art education. So he took two skeins of wool from the dyeing shop, one was reddish and the other one sort of green; then he asked me and I answered . . . and called the red one green and vice versa. That put an end to my career . . .

STRANGER: But that's only fair.

HOUSE-
PAINTER: No, because the thing is, you see, I could distinguish between the colours but not the names. That was only discovered when I was thirty-seven . . .

STRANGER: That's a sad story, but I didn't know any better . . . please forgive me.

HOUSE-
PAINTER: How can I?

STRANGER: My ignorance is my excuse. Listen . . . I was going to join the navy. I had a go as a cadet but became sea-sick and that was it. I was dismissed. But I was a good sailor, it's just that I had drunk too much the night before. So my future was ruined and I had to choose another career . . .

HOUSE-
PAINTER: What have I got to do with the navy? I dreamt of Rome and Paris . . .

STRANGER: Well, we all dream so much when we're young, and when we're old too. Anyway, that was a long time ago, it's not worth talking about now.

HOUSE-
PAINTER: How can you say that? Can you give me back my life . . .

STRANGER: No, I can't but you can't blame me for that. I'd learnt about the wool at school and you ought to have known the names of the colours. Why don't you make yourself scarce . . . I'm sure the world can do with a dauber less. There is Mrs Vesterlund.

HOUSE-
PAINTER :   You don't half talk. But your turn will come.

                 Mrs Vesterlund enters.

STRANGER :   How do you do, Mrs Vesterlund, it's me, Arvid, don't
                 be afraid. I've been in America, how are you? I'm fine
                 and you've had a fire, I see. Your husband is dead, he
                 was a very decent policeman, I liked him because he was
                 always in such a good mood. And he had such a friendly
                 manner, yes, he was a harmless wit who never hurt anyone.
                 I remember once . . .

MRS
VESTERLUND: Oh, my god. I do believe it's my little Arvid whom I
                 used to look after . . .

STRANGER :   No, you used to look after my brother, but never mind,
                 I was talking about your husband who died thirty-five
                 years ago, he was a kind man, a very special friend of
                 mine . . .

MRS
VESTERLUND: Yes, he died, *(Pause)* but I don't know . . . maybe you
                 mix him up with . . .

STRANGER :   I'm not mixing anyone up with old Mr Vesterlund. I
                 remember him well and I liked him a lot . . .

MRS
VESTERLUND: *(Slowly)* I know one shouldn't say this, but he wasn't
                 very good-tempered, really.

STRANGER :   Wasn't he?

MRS
VESTERLUND: Well, he had a way of ingratiating himself with people,
                 but he didn't mean what he said . . . or he said it back
                 to front so to speak . . .

STRANGER :   What? Didn't he mean what he said? Was he false in
                 other words?

MRS
VESTERLUND: To my shame, I must admit . . .

STRANGER :   Wasn't he honest?

MRS
VESTERLUND: Hm. He . . . was . . . a little . . . well, he didn't mean
what he said. But tell me, sir, how have you been
keeping?

STRANGER : Now I see . . . What a serpent! And I have spoken well
of him for over thirty-five years. I've missed him,
almost grieved for him, I bought a funeral wreath for
his coffin with my tobacco money . . .

MRS
VESTERLUND: What was it, what was it then?

STRANGER : What a two-faced bastard! *(Pause)* Well, he cheated me
one Shrove Tuesday . . . he told me that if you took
away every third egg from the hens they'd lay more
eggs. I took his advice, was given a hiding and nearly
ended up in court . . . but I never suspected that he
was the informer . . . he used to come begging in the
kitchen and he saw through his fingers when the maids
poured out the slop any hour of the day . . . now I see
him in his true light. And here I am, getting angry
with someone who's been buried for thirty-five years.
So he didn't mean what he said, he was ironic in other
words . . . I didn't understand at the time. But now I
do.

MRS
VESTERLUND: Yes, he was always a bit of a joker, that's for sure.

STRANGER : Now it all comes back to me . . . and I've spoken well
of that fool for thirty-five years. I attended his funeral,
was offered my first strong drink . . . and I remember
how he used to flatter me, he called me the professor,
the boss . . . oh how awful. Here comes the stone-
mason. You'd better go inside or there'll be a quarrel
when he turns up with his bills; good-bye, madam. We
shall meet again.

MRS
VESTERLUND: *(Goes inside.)* No, we shall not meet again, one should
never meet again, it's not the same as the first time, it
only spoils things, why did you have to mention all that
. . . I was so happy . . .

  The Stone-mason enters.

STRANGER: Come here.

STONE-
MASON: What's that?

STRANGER: Come on. *(The Stone-mason stares at him.)* Are you looking at my tie pin? I bought it in London, at Charing Cross.

STONE-
MASON: I'm not a thief.

STRANGER: No, but you're practising the noble art of erasing. You erase.

STONE-
MASON: That's true, but it was a false contract which would have been the end of me.

STRANGER: Why did you sign it then?

STONE-
MASON: Because I was in trouble.

STRANGER: That's a motive.

STONE-
MASON: But now I've had my revenge.

STRANGER: I'm glad to hear it.

STONE-
MASON: And they have to turn up!

STRANGER: Did we never use to fight as boys?

STONE-
MASON: No, I was too young.

STRANGER: Have we never lied about each other, stolen anything, or crossed each other's paths or seduced each other's sisters?

STONE-
MASON: No, but my father worked at the customs office and your father was a smuggler, sir . . .

STRANGER: Ah well, we do have something in common then, after all.

STONE-
MASON: But when my father didn't want to get involved he was
          given the sack.

STRANGER: Are you going to take it out on me . . . that your father
          was a fool?

STONE-
MASON: Why did you say that there was dynamite in the cellar?

STRANGER: You're lying again. I said there might be dynamite in
          the cellar, everything is possible, after all.

STONE-
MASON: Now the student has been arrested. Do you know him?

STRANGER: Very superficially. His mother worked as a maid in
          your house. She was a beautiful and good woman. I
          asked her to marry me, in the meantime she had a
          child.

STONE-
MASON: Aren't you the father of that child then?

STRANGER: No. But as paternity can't be denied I suppose I'm the
          stepfather.

STONE-
MASON: So people have been lying about you?

STRANGER: Of course. But that's nothing new . . .

STONE-
MASON: And I was one of the people who testified against you,
          on oath.

STRANGER: That doesn't surprise me. But it doesn't matter.
          Nothing matters any longer. Now let's stop bringing up
          unpleasant things from the past or we'll end up in a
          hopeless mess like in that old nursery rhyme.

STONE-
MASON: But I've committed perjury.

STRANGER: Yes, it's not very nice, but things like that do happen
          . . .

STONE-
MASON: It's awful. Isn't it awful to be alive?

STRANGER: *(Covering his eyes with his hands.)* Yes, it's indescribably awful.

STONE-
MASON: I don't want to live any longer . . .

STRANGER: You have to. *(Pause)* You have to. *(Pause)* Listen, they've arrested the student, can he be released?

STONE-
MASON: It's not easy. I'll tell you something while we're on the subject: he's innocent, but he can't be released because the only person who can prove his innocence must needs prove his guilt in another matter.

STRANGER: The one with the hairpins?

STONE-
MASON: Yes.

STRANGER: The old one or the young one?

STONE-
MASON: You'll have to work that one out for yourself, but it's not the cook, that much I can tell you.

STRANGER: What a tapestry! But who put the lamp there?

STONE-
MASON: His worst enemy.

STRANGER: Did his worst enemy start the fire too?

STONE-
MASON: That I don't know. Only the bricklayer knows that.

STRANGER: Who's the bricklayer?

STONE-
MASON: He's the oldest person around here, a distant relative of Mrs Vesterlund; he knows all the secrets about this house, he's conspired with the ironmonger so he won't testify.

STRANGER: Who's this wife of the ironmonger, my sister-in-law?

STONE-
MASON: She was a governess until the last wife left.

STRANGER: What's her character like?

STONE-MASON:	Hm. Character? I don't know what you mean by that, sir. Do you mean profession? Name and status as it says on the census register, but by that they mean occupation.
STRANGER:	I mean temperament.
STONE-MASON:	I see, well, temperament is not something static. As far as I'm concerned it depends who I'm talking to. If I'm talking to a friendly person I'm friendly back but with a vicious person I become like a wild animal.
STRANGER:	We were talking about my sister-in-law's temperament in general.
STONE-MASON:	Yes . . . well, nothing much . . . like most people, I suppose. She gets angry if you tease her, and then she's sweet again. After all, we can't be good-tempered all the time.
STRANGER:	I mean is she happy or melancholy by nature?
STONE-MASON:	When things are going well she is happy and when things are going against her she is sad or angry, like the rest of us.
STRANGER:	Yes, but what is her nature?
STONE-MASON:	That's one and the same thing, isn't it? But as she's an educated person she is well-mannered, but . . . on the other hand, she can be coarse, when she sets her mind to it.
STRANGER:	I'm none the wiser for that.
STONE-MASON:	*(Pats his shoulder.)* No, that's a true word, you're never the wiser where people are concerned, sir.
STRANGER:	Not a fool, this chap. How do you like my brother, the ironmonger?

       Pause.

STONE-
MASON: He's got nice manners. That's all I can say, because I
    can't judge what I can't see.

STRANGER: Excellent. He's always got blue hands, but you know
    that they are white underneath, don't you?

STONE-
MASON: We need to scrape them off first, but he won't allow
    that.

STRANGER: Good. Who is this young couple coming here?

STONE-
MASON: It's Gustavsson's son and my daughter. They were
    going to get married tonight, but the marriage has been
    postponed because of the fire. I've got to go now
    because I don't want to embarrass them. Good-bye.
    (Exits)

    *Stranger withdraws behind the inn, but remains visible
    to the audience.*

    Alfred and Matilda enter, holding hands.

ALFRED: I had to come here and look at the scene of the fire. I
    had to . . .

MATILDA: What's there to look at?

ALFRED: I've suffered so much in this house that I've often
    wished it would burn down . . .

MATILDA: Yes, I knew it was shading the garden and now it will
    grow much better as long as they don't build a new and
    bigger house in its place . . .

ALFRED: It's a lovely plot of land with a nice sunny aspect and
    I've heard that there's going to be a street here . . .

MATILDA: So you may move away?

ALFRED: Yes, we're all going to move away . . . I like that, I like
    new things. I'd like to emigrate really . . .

MATILDA: Oh no. Did you know that our pigeons had built nests
    in the roof and last night when the fire started they
    circled around at first and then they headed straight for
    the fire. They couldn't part from their old home, you
    see.

ALFRED: We must get away from here . . . away! Father says
            that this soil is completely drained of nourishment . . .

MATILDA: I heard that they were going to take the cinders to the
            plantations to improve the soil there . . .

ALFRED: You mean the ashes . . .

MATILDA: Yes, I've heard that it's good to mix in ashes . . .

ALFRED: New topsoil is better . . .

MATILDA: But your father is a ruined man now . . .

ALFRED: Not at all, he's got money in the bank. Yes, I know he
            complains but so does everybody, don't they?

MATILDA: Has he . . . isn't he ruined after the fire?

ALFRED: Not a bit. He is a cunning old devil although he calls
            himself a fool . . .

MATILDA: What am I to believe?

ALFRED: He has lent some money to the bricklayer and to
            several others too.

MATILDA: I don't know where I am. Am I dreaming? We've been
            crying the whole morning about your father's
            misfortune and about the postponed wedding . . .

ALFRED: Poor you. But we're going to have the wedding tonight
            . . .

MATILDA: Is it not postponed?

ALFRED: It is postponed by two hours . . . until father can get
            hold of a new coat.

MATILDA: And we who cried . . .

ALFRED: Vain tears. So many tears.

MATILDA: It annoys me that they were in vain, but . . . how can
            he play such a dirty trick on us?

ALFRED: He's a bit of a joker, that's true. He always complains
            of being so tired too, but it's just laziness, he's so lazy,
            so lazy . . .

MATILDA: Don't say any more bad things about him now, but
            let's get away from here – I must get dressed and put

my hair up. I can't get over the fact that father-in-law isn't the person I thought he was. Fancy playing games and cheating us like that. Perhaps you're like that as well. I don't know you, either.

ALFRED: You will . . . soon enough.

MATILDA: When it's too late . . .

ALFRED: It's never too late . . .

MATILDA: You're so vicious around here and now I'm afraid of you . . .

ALFRED: Surely not of me . . .

MATILDA: I don't know what to believe . . . why didn't you tell me that father-in-law was well-off?

ALFRED: I wanted to test you, to see if you liked me even if I didn't have any money.

MATILDA: That's what they say afterwards . . . they just wanted to test you. But that means that I can never believe in a person again.

ALFRED: Go and get changed now. I'll order the carriages . . .

MATILDA: Are we going to have carriages?

ALFRED: Yes, of course. Covered carriages.

MATILDA: Covered? And this evening? Oh, how fun! Come, come quickly! We're going to have covered carriages.

ALFRED: *(Takes her hand and they skip out.)* Here I am, all yours! Whoopee.

STRANGER: Bravo.

> *The plain clothes policeman enters, speaks slowly to the stranger who answers in the same way for about half a minute and after that the policeman leaves again.*

SISTER-IN-
LAW: *(Enters, dressed in black, stares at the Stranger for a long time.)* Are you my brother-in-law?

STRANGER: Yes. *(Pause)* Do I not correspond to the description – or depiction perhaps?

SISTER-IN-
LAW: To be honest, no.

STRANGER: As a rule, one doesn't. And I must confess that the
                description I've just had of your character doesn't
                correspond to the original, either.

SISTER-IN-
LAW: People hurt each other so much and they change each
                other, every one according to their own image . . .

STRANGER: And they walk about like theatre directors and dish out
                parts to each other; some accept their part, others
                refuse it and prefer to improvise . . .

SISTER-IN-
LAW: What have you been type-cast as, then?

STRANGER: The seducer. Not because I've been a seducer. I've
                never seduced anyone, neither a young girl nor
                someone else's wife but once in my youth I was
                seduced . . . that's how I got the part. It was forced
                upon me so I had to accept it. And for twenty years
                I've been walking around with the bad conscience of a
                seducer . . .

SISTER-IN-
LAW: So you were innocent?

STRANGER: Oh yes.

SISTER-IN-
LAW: How strange. My husband still talks about Divine
                Nemesis who's pursued you because you seduced
                another man's wife once.

STRANGER: I believe you. But you see, your husband is a more
                interesting case. He's made up a character for himself,
                he's said that he's a coward when it comes to life's
                battles, hasn't he?

SISTER-IN-
LAW: Yes, he is a coward alright.

STRANGER: But he boasts about his courage which is nothing but
                brutality.

SISTER-IN-
LAW: You know him well.

STRANGER: Yes and no. Have you been under the delusion that you married into a respectable family whose honour is above reproach?

SISTER-IN-
LAW: That's what I believed until this morning.

STRANGER: And then it fell apart. What a tapestry of lies, mistakes, misunderstandings. And we're supposed to take this seriously?

SISTER-IN-
LAW: Do you?

STRANGER: Sometimes. Very rarely, nowadays. I'm like a sleepwalker walking on a cornice . . . I know I'm asleep but I'm awake . . . I'm just waiting to be woken up.

SISTER-IN-
LAW: You may have been on the other side . . .

STRANGER: I've crossed the river, but I remember nothing about it, except that everything over there was what it claimed to be. That's the difference.

SISTER-IN-
LAW: When things break at the touch what shall we hold on to?

STRANGER: Don't you know?

SISTER-IN-
LAW: No, tell me. Tell me.

STRANGER: Sorrow breeds patience, patience breeds skill, skill gives hope, and hope's not put to shame.

SISTER-IN-
LAW: Hope, yes.

STRANGER: Yes, hope.

SISTER-IN-
LAW: Don't you ever enjoy life?

STRANGER: Of course, but even that's an illusion. I'll tell you, my dear sister-in-law that when you've been born without a film over your eyes you see life and people as they really are . . . one has to be a pig to enjoy this sludge. And when one's had enough dust in one's eyes, one turns one's eyes inside out and peers into the soul. That's something worth looking at . . .

SISTER-IN-LAW: What do you see there?

STRANGER: You see yourself. But when you've seen yourself, you must die.

SISTER-IN-LAW: *(Covering her eyes. Pause.)* Do you want to help me?

STRANGER: If I can.

SISTER-IN-LAW: Please try!

STRANGER: Wait a minute! No, I can't. He's been wrongfully arrested, only you can set him free, but you can't do that. This is not a net spun by humans. . . .

SISTER-IN-LAW: But he's not guilty.

STRANGER: Who is guilty then?

Pause.

SISTER-IN-LAW: Nobody! The fire was an accident.

STRANGER: I know.

SISTER-IN-LAW: What shall I do?

STRANGER: Suffer. It will pass. Even that is vanity.

SISTER-IN-LAW: Suffer?

STRANGER: Suffer, yes. But keep on hoping.

SISTER-IN-LAW: *(Holding out her hand.)* Thank you.

STRANGER: And as a consolation . . .

SISTER-IN-LAW: What?

STRANGER: You're not alone in suffering without cause.

> *She turns her head and walks away. The Stranger steps onto the ruins.*

IRON-
MONGER: *(Enters, happy.)* Are you playing ghosts here on the ruins?

STRANGER: Ghosts like ruins. You're happy?

IRON-
MONGER: Yes, now I'm happy.

STRANGER: And brave?

IRON-
MONGER: What or who have I to fear?

STRANGER: I can see from your happy face that you're ignorant of one important factor. Have you got enough courage to face another setback?

IRON-
MONGER: What's it about?

STRANGER: You're turning pale.

IRON-
MONGER: Am I?

STRANGER: A great setback.

IRON-
MONGER: Tell me!

STRANGER: A plain clothes' policeman was here just now and he told me . . .

IRON-
MONGER: What?

STRANGER: That the insurance money was handed over two hours too late . . .

IRON-
MONGER: What on . . . what are you saying? But I sent my wife with the money.

STRANGER: And she sent the book-keeper . . . and he arrived too late.

IRON-
MONGER: Then I'm ruined.

Pause.

STRANGER: Are you crying?

IRON-
MONGER: I'm ruined.

STRANGER: Yes. Is it too much to bear?

IRON-
MONGER: What shall I live on? What shall I do?

STRANGER: Work!

IRON-
MONGER: I'm too old, I haven't got any friends . . .

STRANGER: Maybe you'll get some now. An unhappy person is
always attractive . . . I had my best moments in
adversity.

IRON-
MONGER: *(Wild)* I'm ruined.

STRANGER: But when things went well for me and when fortune
smiled I was alone; envy couldn't hide under friendship
. . .

IRON-
MONGER: I'll sue the book-keeper.

STRANGER: Don't do that.

IRON-
MONGER: He'll have to find the money.

STRANGER: You haven't changed at all. What's the point of living if
you don't learn anything from life?

IRON-
MONGER: I'll sue him, he was a thief, he hated me because I hit
him once . . .

STRANGER: Forgive him – like I did when I remitted my
inheritance to you.

IRON-
MONGER: Which inheritance?

STRANGER: Incorrigible, merciless, cowardly, mendacious. Go in
peace, brother.

IRON-
MONGER: Which inheritance are you talking about?

STRANGER: Listen, brother Rudolf . . . my mother's son in any case
             . . . you got the stone-mason framed because he erased
             . . . well . . . but you erased my name in 'Christopher
             Columbus or the Discoverer of America' . . .

IRON-
MONGER: *(Surprised)* What, what, what . . .? Columbus?

STRANGER: Yes, my book which became yours. *(Ironmonger doesn't
             answer.)* Yes. And now I understand why you put the
             lamp in the student's wardrobe, I understand
             everything, but did you know that our dining-table was
             not made of ebony?

IRON-
MONGER: Wasn't it?

STRANGER: No, it was maple wood.

IRON-
MONGER: Maple?

STRANGER: The glory and pride of our home, valued at 2000
             kronor.

IRON-
MONGER: That too . . . a bluff?

STRANGER: Yes.

IRON-
MONGER: Oh, dear.

STRANGER: The debt is settled, the case written off, the matter
             cannot be solved, the parties secede. . . .

IRON-
MONGER: *(Rushes out.)* I'm ruined.

STRANGER: *(Picks up his wreath from the table.)* I was going to the
             cemetery with this wreath to put it on the parents'
             grave, but I'll put it here instead, on the ruins of my
             parents' home, the home of my childhood. *(Says a
             silent prayer.)* And now: out into the wide world again,
             wanderer!

THE END

Opus 3
THE GHOST SONATA

CHARACTERS

THE OLD MAN	(Mr Hummel)
UNDERGRADUATE	(Mr Arkenholz)
MILKMAID	(A vision)
CONCIERGE	(Female)
THE DEAD CONSUL	
THE DARK LADY	(The consul's daughter with the concierge)
THE COLONEL	
THE MUMMY	(The colonel's wife)
HIS DAUGHTER	(Who is really the old man's daughter)
NOBLEMAN	(Called Baron Skanskorg, betrothed to the concierge's daughter)
JOHANSSON	(Hummel's servant)
BENGTSSON	(The colonel's servant)
THE FIANCÉE	(Hummel's ex-fiancée, a white-haired old woman)
THE COOK	

SCENE ONE

The ground floor and the first floor of an apartment block, but only the corner of the building which finishes in a round drawing-room on the ground floor and a balcony with a flag-pole on the first floor is visible to the audience.

When the roller blind is taken up in the round drawing-room we see a white marble statue of a young woman surrounded by palms: the statue is in strong sunlight which is coming through the open windows. On the window-sill, to the left are pots of hyacinths (blue, white and pink.)

On the balcony rail, a blue silk quilt and two white pillows are spread out to air. The windows to the left are covered with white sheets.

It is a clear Sunday morning.

In front of the house, in the foreground, stands a green bench. To the right, in the foreground, a street fountain, to the left, a hoarding.

To the left, at the back is the main entrance to the building revealing a staircase of white marble, a banister of mahogany and brass; on both sides of the entrance door there are bay-leaf trees placed in tubs on the pavement.

The corner with its round drawing-room also faces a side street which is presumed to lead to the back.

To the left of the entrance door, on the ground floor a window with a window-mirror.

As the curtain rises we can hear several church bells ringing in the distance.

The doors into the building are open. A woman dressed in dark clothes stands immobile on the stairs.

The Woman Concierge sweeps the porch; then she rubs the brass fittings on the door and finally she waters the bay trees. In a wheel-chair beside the hoarding the Old Man sits reading his paper. He is white-haired with a beard and he wears spectacles.

The Milkmaid enters from the corner with bottles in a wire basket; she is dressed in summer clothes with brown shoes, black stockings and a white cap; she takes the cap off and puts it on the fountain; wipes the sweat from her brow; drinks from her scoop; washes her hands; arranges her hair, looks at the reflection of her face in the water.

The bell from a steamer and the bass from an organ in a nearby church break through the silence now and again.

After a few minutes, when the girl has finished her toilette, the Undergraduate enters from the left, looking tired and unkempt. He walks straight up to the fountain.

        Pause.

STUDENT: May I borrow your scoop? *(The girl snatches her scoop.)* Haven't you finished soon?

        The girl looks at him with horror.

OLD MAN: *(To himself.)* Who's he talking to? I can't see anyone. Is the fellow mad?

        Continues to look at them with great surprise.

STUDENT: What are you looking at? Do I look so terrible? You see, I haven't slept all night . . . you obviously think I've been painting the town red . . . *(The girl continues to look at him with horror.)* You think I've been drinking, don't you? Do I smell of arrak? I haven't shaved, I know . . . Give me a drink of water, darling, I've deserved it. *(Pause)* Alright! I'll tell you then: I've bandaged and looked after sick people all night. I was there when that house collapsed last night, you see . . . so now you know. *(The girl rinses the scoop and gives him a drink.)* Thank you. *(The girl immobile. Slowly.)* Would you do me a great favour? *(Pause)* The thing is . . . my eyes are inflamed, as you can see but my hands have been in contact with sick people and dead bodies so I can't touch my eyes without a certain danger . . . Would you please take my clean handkerchief and dip it in the cold water and dab my poor eyes? Would you do that for me? Do you want to be my Good Samaritan? *(The girl hesitates but does what he asks her to do.)* Thank you, my friend. *(Takes up his purse. The girl makes a dismissive gesture.)* Sorry, that was thoughtless of me, I'm not quite awake yet . . .

OLD MAN: *(To the Student.)* Excuse me, but I couldn't help overhearing . . . so you were present at the accident last night . . . I've just been reading about it here in the paper . . .

STUDENT: Is it already in the paper?

OLD MAN: Yes, it's all here; and there's a picture of you too but they regret that they didn't get the name of the clever student who . . .

STUDENT: *(Looks at the newspaper.)* I see. That's me. Hm.

OLD MAN: Who were you talking to just now?

STUDENT: Didn't you see?

       Pause.

OLD MAN: Is it rude to demand . . . to ask your name?

STUDENT: Why? I don't like publicity – if people praise you, they're sure to find fault with you later – the art of belittling is so well developed – besides, I'm not interested in a reward . . .

OLD MAN: Perhaps you're comfortably off?

STUDENT: Not at all. On the contrary, I'm destitute.

OLD MAN: Listen . . . I seem to recognize your voice . . . I once had a friend who couldn't say window . . . he always said 'vindow' . . . I've only met one person with that pronunciation and that was him; the other one is you – is it possible that you're related to Arkenholz, the wholesale dealer?

STUDENT: Yes, he was my father.

OLD MAN: Strange are the paths of fate . . . I saw you once when you were a little boy, under very difficult circumstances . . .

STUDENT: Yes, they say I was born in the middle of bankruptcy proceedings . . .

OLD MAN: That's right.

STUDENT: May I ask what your name is?

OLD MAN: My name is Hummel, I used to be managing director Hummel . . .

STUDENT: Are you . . . I remember now . . .

OLD MAN: You've heard my name mentioned often in your family?

STUDENT: Yes.

OLD MAN: Perhaps with a certain displeasure? *(Student doesn't answer.)* Yes, I can imagine. I suppose they said I ruined your father. Everyone who came a cropper on those stupid speculations blames it on those who weren't so easily duped. *(Pause)* The situation is this . . . your father robbed me of 17,000 *kronor* and that was all my savings in those days.

STUDENT: Isn't it strange how the same story can be told in two such diametrically opposed ways.

OLD MAN: You don't think I'm lying, do you?

STUDENT: I don't know what to think. My father didn't lie, anyway.

OLD MAN: It's true, a father never lies . . . but I'm also a father, so . . .

STUDENT: What are you trying to say?

OLD MAN: I once saved your father from misery and he repaid me with a terrible hatred, that's part of indebtedness . . . he spread lies about me in his family.

STUDENT: Maybe your generosity was poisoned with unnecessary humiliations.

OLD MAN: All help is humiliating, sir.

STUDENT: What do you want from me?

OLD MAN: I don't want any money from you; but if you want to do me some favours I'd be very happy. As you can see I'm a cripple; some say it's my own fault, others blame it on my parents; I think it's life itself with all its snares, because if you try to avoid one you're sure to walk headlong into another one. The fact is, I can't run upstairs, I can't ring bells, so . . . would you please help me?

STUDENT: What can I do?

OLD MAN: First, push me around so I can read the hoardings; I want to see what they're playing tonight . . .

STUDENT: *(Pushes the wheel-chair.)* Haven't you got a servant?

OLD MAN: Yes, but he's just run an errand for me . . . he'll soon
            be back. Are you studying medicine?

STUDENT: No, I read languages, but I don't know what I want to
            do . . .

OLD MAN: I see. Are you good at mathematics?

STUDENT: Quite.

OLD MAN: Good! Are you looking for a job?

STUDENT: Well, why not?

OLD MAN: Good. *(Reads the hoarding.)* There's a matinée
            performance of *The Valkyrie* today . . . the colonel will
            be there with his daughter. He always sits at the end of
            row six so I'll put you beside him . . . would you like
            to go to the telephone kiosk over there and order a ticket
            in row six, number 82?

STUDENT: Am I going to the opera today?

OLD MAN: Yes. And if you do as I ask you, you'll be richly
            rewarded . . . good-bye for now. I want to see you
            happy, rich and respected. Your début last night as the
            brave rescuer will make you famous by tomorrow and
            your name will be worth a lot then.

STUDENT: *(Goes to the telephone kiosk.)* This is a strange encounter
            . . .

OLD MAN: You like a good adventure, don't you?

STUDENT: Yes, that's my misfortune . . .

OLD MAN: . . . which will turn into your fortune. Go on,
            telephone now. *(Reads his paper. The lady dressed in
            dark has come out onto the pavement and is speaking with
            the Concierge; the Old Man is listening but the audience
            cannot hear anything. The Student returns.)* Is it fixed
            up?

STUDENT: It's done.

OLD MAN: Do you see that house?

STUDENT: I've observed it . . . I walked past here yesterday when
            the sun was shining on the windows and I imagined all
            the beautiful and luxurious things in there – and I said

to my friend: What about having a flat there, on the fourth floor with a young wife, two beautiful little children and a private income of 20,000 a year . . .

OLD MAN: Did you say that? Did you say that? I love that house too.

STUDENT: Are you dealing in real estate, by any chance?

OLD MAN: Hmm . . . Not in the way you mean . . .

STUDENT: Do you know the people who live there?

OLD MAN: I know them all. At my age one knows everybody, their fathers and grandfathers, and one is always related to them in some way or other – I've just celebrated my eightieth birthday – but no one knows me, not really – I take an interest in people's destinies . . . *(The roller blind in the round drawing room is taken up. The Colonel can be seen inside, dressed in civilian clothes, after having checked the thermometer he walks back into the room and stops in front of the marble statue.)* Look, there is the colonel whom you're going to sit beside this afternoon . . .

STUDENT: Is that the colonel? I don't understand any of this; it's like a fairy tale . . .

OLD MAN: All my life is like a book of fairy tales, sir. Even though the various fairy tales are quite different there's a leitmotif that runs through it all.

STUDENT: That marble statue in there . . . who is that supposed to be?

OLD MAN: His wife, of course . . .

STUDENT: Was she so adorable?

OLD MAN: Hmm. Yes!

STUDENT: Well? Tell me.

OLD MAN: Adorable? My dear boy, if I tell you that she left him . . . that he hit her and that she went back to him, remarried him and that she's now sitting there like a mummy, worshipping her own statue – then you'll think that I've gone mad, won't you?

STUDENT: I don't understand.

OLD MAN: That's what I thought. And over there's the hyacinth
             window. That's where his daughter lives. She's out
             riding now, but she'll soon be back . . .

STUDENT: Who is the dark lady talking to the concierge?

OLD MAN: Well, it's a little complicated . . . it's to do with the
             dead man upstairs, you see . . . where the white sheets
             are hanging . . .

STUDENT: Who was he then?

OLD MAN: He was a human being like the rest of us but he
             appeared vain most of the time . . . if you were born on
             a Sunday you'd see him coming through those doors
             soon, then he'd look at the flag outside the consulate –
             which is at half mast; he used to be a consul you see
             and he liked crowns, lions, coats of arms, coloured
             ribbons and decorations.

STUDENT: You said 'born on a Sunday'. I actually happen to be
             born on a Sunday . . .

OLD MAN: Really? Well, I never . . . I could tell from the colour
             of your eyes . . . then you can see what others can't.
             Are you aware of that?

STUDENT: I don't know what others can see, but sometimes . . .
             no, one doesn't talk about things like that.

OLD MAN: I almost knew it. But you can tell me . . . because I
             . . . understand things like that.

STUDENT: Yesterday, for instance . . . I was drawn to that obscure
             street where the house later collapsed . . . I arrived
             there and I stopped outside a building which I'd never
             seen before . . . then I noticed a crack in the wall, I
             heard the floors creaking; I ran up to the house and
             snatched one of the children who was walking under
             the wall . . . at the next moment the house fell down
             . . . I escaped but in my arms – where I thought I was
             carrying the child – there was nothing . . .

OLD MAN: I say . . . I thought . . . tell me: why did you
             gesticulate like that just now in front of the fountain?
             And why did you talk to yourself?

STUDENT: Didn't you see the milkmaid I was talking to?

OLD MAN: *(Horrified)* The milkmaid?

STUDENT: Yes, the one who gave me the scoop.

OLD MAN: I see. That's how it is. Well, I don't have second sight
            but I have other talents . . . *(A white-haired woman sits
            down beside the mirror at the window.)* Look at that old
            woman at the window. Can you see her? She used to
            be my fiancée once, sixty years ago. I was twenty then.
            Don't worry, she doesn't recognize me. We see each
            other every day, but she doesn't make the least
            impression on me . . . even though we swore eternal
            fidelity once . . . eternal.

STUDENT: How silly you were in your generation. We don't talk
            about things like that with our girlfriends.

OLD MAN: I'm sorry, but we didn't know any better. But can you
            imagine that old lady being young and beautiful once?

STUDENT: No, I can't. Yes, she's got a beautiful expression, but I
            can't see her eyes . . .

            *The Concierge enters with a basket and strews fir twigs
            on the ground.*

OLD MAN: The concierge, yes. The dark lady over there is her
            daughter and the dead man was her father; that's why
            the man was offered the job as concierge . . . but the
            dark lady has a beau who comes from a good family
            and who is expecting a fortune; he is in the process of
            divorcing his wife who'll give him a substantial house
            just to get rid of him. This smart gentleman is the dead
            man's son-in-law; you can see his bed clothes hanging
            out to air up there on the balcony . . . It's complicated,
            as you can see.

STUDENT: It's damned complicated.

OLD MAN: Yes, that's how it is, inside and out . . . even though it
            looks so simple.

STUDENT: But who was the dead man then?

OLD MAN: You asked me that just now and I told you: if you
            could see round the corner where the servants' entrance
            is you'd notice a crowd of poor people who've been
            helped by him . . . whenever it suited him . . .

STUDENT: So he was a good person then?

OLD MAN: Sometimes.

STUDENT: Not always?

OLD MAN: No. That's the way people are. Listen, young man, could you push me a bit into the sun, do you think, I'm so cold. When you sit still all the time your blood stiffens – I'll probably die soon . . . I know I will, but before I do, I have a few things to do – feel my hand, can you feel how cold I am.

STUDENT: That's not normal. *(Moves away.)*

OLD MAN: Don't leave me, I'm tired and lonely but it hasn't always been like this. I have a very long life behind me – very long – I've made people unhappy and people have made me unhappy, one cancels out the other . . . but before I die I want to make you happy . . . our destinies are interwoven through your father . . . and other things . . .

STUDENT: Let go of my hand, you take all my strength away, you make me cold, what do you want?

OLD MAN: Be patient and you'll see. Here's the young lady . . .

STUDENT: The colonel's daughter?

OLD MAN: Yes. Daughter. Look at her. Have you ever seen such a masterpiece?

STUDENT: She's like the marble statue in there . . .

OLD MAN: That's her mother.

STUDENT: You're right – I've never seen such a woman of woman born – happy the man who can lead her to the altar and to his home.

OLD MAN: You see that, do you? Everyone doesn't appreciate her beauty. Well, it is written . . . *(Young lady enters from left in a fashionable English riding habit, walks slowly and without looking at anyone up to the door where she stops and exchanges a few words with the Concierge: then she disappears into the house. The Student covers his eyes with his hands.)* Are you crying?

STUDENT: When faced with a hopeless case I feel despair.

OLD MAN: I can open doors and hearts as long as I have an arm at
            my disposal . . . If you help me I'll let you rule . . .

STUDENT: Is that a deal? Do I have to sell my soul?

OLD MAN: Nothing to sell. You see, I have taken . . . all my life
            I've taken; now I have a desire to give, give. But no
            one wants to receive . . . I'm a rich man, very rich, but
            I have no heirs, yes, one reptile who torments me to
            death . . . do you want to become like a son to me,
            inherit my wealth while I'm still alive, enjoy yourself
            while I can still watch you, from a distance.

STUDENT: What do you want me to do?

OLD MAN: Go and listen to *The Valkyrie* first.

STUDENT: That's already arranged, what else?

OLD MAN: This evening I want you to sit in there, in the round
            drawing-room.

STUDENT: How am I going to get in there?

OLD MAN: Through *The Valkyrie*.

STUDENT: Why have you chosen me to be your go-between? Did
            you know me before?

OLD MAN: Of course. I've had my eyes on you for a long time . . .
            But look there, on the balcony, look how the maid
            hoists the flag at half-mast for the consul . . . and then
            she turns the bed clothes over . . . can you see the blue
            quilt? It used to be for two people, but now it's only
            for one . . . *(The young lady reappears in different
            clothes, she's watering her hyacinths in the window.)*
            There's my little girl, look at her, look. She's talking to
            the flowers, like a blue hyacinth herself, isn't she? She
            gives them clean water to drink . . . and they turn the
            water into colours and scents . . . here comes the
            colonel with his newspaper. He shows her the house
            that collapsed . . . now he's pointing at the photograph
            of you. She is not indifferent exactly . . . she reads
            about your bravery. I think it's clouding over, what if it
            starts to rain, then I'm truly stuck unless Johansson
            comes back soon . . . *(It is getting overcast and it is
            becoming darker. The old lady by her mirror shuts the
            window.)* Now my fiancée is closing the window . . .

seventy-nine . . . that mirror is the only one she uses because she can't see herself in that one, only the outside world and from two directions at that, but the world can see her . . . she hasn't thought of that . . . not a bad-looking old lady, really . . .

The dead man can be seen walking into the street in his shroud.

STUDENT: My God, what do I see?

OLD MAN: What do you see?

STUDENT: Don't you see . . . outside the main door . . . the dead man?

OLD MAN: I can't see anything, but I expected something. Tell me . . .

STUDENT: He's walking into the street . . . *(Pause)* Now he's turning his head and looking at the flag.

OLD MAN: What did I say? He'll soon be counting the wreaths as well, and reading the cards of condolence . . . it won't be easy for those who've forgotten to send any.

STUDENT: Now he's going round the corner . . .

OLD MAN: He's going to count the poor people at the servants' entrance . . . the poor are such a good backcloth: "accompanied by the blessings from the many," yes, but I won't give him my blessing. Between ourselves, he was a real blood-sucker . . .

STUDENT: But charitable . . .

OLD MAN: A charitable barbarian who was always planning a handsome funeral . . . when he felt his life was drawing to an end he robbed the state of 50,000 *kronor* . . . and now his daughter is walking into someone else's marriage wondering about her inheritance . . . that bastard can hear everything we say, but I don't mind. here's Johansson. *(Johansson enters from left.)* Report to base! *(Johansson talks to him but we can't hear what he says.)* I see . . . not at home? You're a fool. And the telegraph? Nothing! Carry on! Six o'clock this evening? Good. Extra edition? His whole name . . . Arkenholz, undergraduate, born . . . parents . . . excellent . . . I

think it's beginning to rain . . . what did he say? I see,
I see. He didn't want to. But he'll have to! Here is our
noble friend. Push me round the corner, Johansson, so
I can hear what the poor people are saying . . . and you
wait for me here, Arkenholz, do you understand?
Hurry, up, hurry up!

Johansson pushes his wheel-chair round the corner.

*Student stays behind, looking at the young lady who is now
weeding her flower pots.*

THE
NOBLEMAN: *(Enters dressed in mourning, addresses the dark lady who
has stepped onto the pavement.)* Yes, what can one do
about that? We'll just have to wait.

LADY: I can't wait.

NOBLEMAN: Is that so? Go to a place in the country then.

LADY: I don't want to.

NOBLEMAN: Come closer or they'll hear what we're saying.

*They move to the hoarding and continue their
conversation there, inaudibly.*

JOHANSSON: *(Enters from right; to the Student.)* My master asked me
to remind you of . . . the other thing.

STUDENT: *(Slowly)* Listen . . . first tell me who your master is.

JOHANSSON: He's so many things, and he's been everything.

STUDENT: Is he sane?

JOHANSSON: What does that mean? All his life he's been looking for
a Sunday child, he says, but it doesn't necessarily have
to be true . . .

STUDENT: What does he want? Is he greedy?

JOHANSSON: He wants to rule . . . All day long he travels around in
his chair like the god Thor . . . he looks at houses, pulls
them down, opens streets, builds squares; but he also
breaks into houses, crawls in through windows, plays
havoc with people's lives, kills his enemies – and never
forgives anyone. Can you imagine that that cripple was
a Don Juan once but he always lost his women.

STUDENT: Why?

JOHANSSON: He is so cunning that he manages to make the women
            leave him as soon as he grows tired of them. But now
            he's like a horse thief at a human fair, he steals people,
            in more ways than one . . . I was practically snatched
            from the arms of justice . . . I had committed a . . .
            blunder, you see, which he alone knew about; instead
            of having me locked up he made me into his slave; I
            slave for my board – which is not even that good . . .

STUDENT: What does he want to do in this house then?

JOHANSSON: I don't want to tell . . . It's so involved.

STUDENT: I think I'll get away from here . . .

JOHANSSON: Look at the young lady, she dropped her bracelet
            through the window . . . *(Student approaches her slowly,
            picks up her bracelet and hands it to her. She thanks him
            in a restrained way. The Student returns to Johansson.)* I
            see, you intend to leave . . . that won't be easy once
            he's got his claws into you . . . and he's not afraid of
            anything between heaven and earth . . . yes, one thing,
            or one person rather . . .

STUDENT: Wait a minute, I think I know.

JOHANSSON: How can you know?

STUDENT: I can guess. He's afraid of a . . . little milkmaid?

JOHANSSON: He always turns away when he sees a milk cart . . . and
            he talks in his sleep, he's been to Hamburg once, I
            think . . .

STUDENT: Can we believe what he says?

JOHANSSON: Everything is possible with that man.

STUDENT: What's he doing around the corner now?

JOHANSSON: He's listening to the poor people . . . he sows a word
            here and there, removes stones, one at a time, until the
            house falls down . . . figuratively speaking . . . You see,
            I'm an educated man, I've been a bookseller once . . .
            are you going?

STUDENT: I find it hard to be ungrateful . . . this man has saved my father from ruin once and now he's just asking me for a small favour in return . . .

JOHANSSON: And what's that?

STUDENT: He wants me to go to the Opera to see *The Valkyrie* . . .

JOHANSSON: I don't understand . . . but he always has these new ideas . . . look at him now . . . he's talking to the policeman . . . he's always mixing with the police, rings them up, gets involved with them, gives them false promises and . . . and in the meantime he is squeezing facts out of them. I promise you . . . before evening he'll be received in the round drawing-room.

STUDENT: What does he want to do there? What's his involvement with the colonel?

JOHANSSON: I have my suspicions, but I'm not sure. You'll see for yourself, when you get there.

STUDENT: I'll never get in there . . .

JOHANSSON: That depends on you. Go to *The Valkyrie* . . .

STUDENT: Is that the way?

JOHANSSON: Yes, if he says so. Look, look at him, look at his battleship, towed in triumph by the beggars who won't get an *öre* in wages, only a hint at some reward after he's dead.

OLD MAN: *(Enters standing up in his wheelchair, pulled by a beggar, followed by others.)* Praise the young man, who risked his own life to save many others' at the accident yesterday. Hail, Arkenholz! *(The Beggars doff their caps but say nothing. The Lady in the window waves with her handkerchief. The Colonel stares out of his window. The Old Lady rises at her window. The Maid on the balcony hoists the flag all the way to the top.)* Clap your hands, citizens, it may be Sunday, but the ass in the well and the corn in the field give us absolution and even though I'm not a Sunday child myself I can still predict what's going to happen and I have healing powers. I resuscitated a drowned person once . . . yes, it was in Hamburg, one Sunday morning just like today . . .

> *(The Milkmaid enters, only seen by the Student and the Old Man; she raises her arms like a drowning person and she stares at the Old Man. Old Man sits down, slumps forward in fright.)* Johansson! Take me away from here! Quickly! Arkenholz, don't forget *The Valkyrie!*

STUDENT: What's the meaning of all this?

JOHANSSON: We'll see. We'll see.

SCENE TWO

Inside the round drawing-room; at the back, a white tiled stove with a mirror, a clock and candelabra; to the right, the hall with a view of a green room with mahogany furniture; to the left stands the statue shaded by palm trees. It can also be concealed by drapes; to the left, at the back a door leading to the hyacinth room where the young lady is sitting reading a book. We can see the Colonel's back where he sits reading in the green room.

Bengtsson, the man-servant, in uniform, enters from the hall with Johansson who is dressed in tails with a white cravat.

BENGTSSON: You can serve, Johansson, while I take care of the clothes. Have you done it before?

JOHANSSON: As you know, I wheel a tank around in the daytime, but in the evenings I serve at parties and it's always been a dream of mine to get into this house . . . they're strange people, aren't they?

BENGTSSON: Yes, a little unusual, I must admit.

JOHANSSON: Is it a musical recital or what?

BENGTSSON: It's the usual ghost supper, as we call it. They drink tea, don't utter a word. Or only the colonel speaks; then they munch their little cakes and biscuits, all at the same time, like mice in an attic room.

JOHANSSON: Why is it called the ghost supper?

BENGTSSON: They look like ghosts . . . and they've been doing it for twenty years now, always the same people who say the same thing. Or they keep quiet so as not to make fools of themselves.

JOHANSSON: Isn't there a wife in the house as well?

BENGTSSON: Oh yes, but she's a bit funny in the head; she spends all her time in a wardrobe because her eyes can't stand the light . . . she's sitting in there . . .

Points to a door covered with wall-paper.

JOHANSSON: In there?

BENGTSSON: Yes, I did say they're a little unusual . . .

JOHANSSON: How does she look?

BENGTSSON: Like a mummy . . . do you want to have a look at her? *(Opens the wall-papered door.)* There she is!

JOHANSSON: Good Lord . . .

THE MUMMY: *(In a baby voice.)* Why do you have to open the door. Haven't I told you to keep the door shut . . .

BENGTSSON: *(Also in a baby voice.)* Ta, ta, ta, ta! Little lolly be a good girl now and she'll get something really nice. Pretty Polly.

THE MUMMY: *(Like a parrot.)* Pretty Polly! Is Jacob there? Crrrrr!

BENGTSSON: She thinks she's a parrot and it's not entirely beyond the realms of possibility . . . *(To the Mummy.)* Polly, whistle for us, please.

The Mummy whistles.

JOHANSSON: I've seen a lot in my days but never anything like this.

BENGTSSON: You see, when a house gets old, it gets mouldy and when people stay together tormenting each other for a long time, they go mad. The wife in this house – shhh Polly! – this mummy has been sitting here for forty years – the same husband, the same furniture, the same relatives, the same friends . . . *(Shuts the door to the Mummy.)* And what's passed in this house . . . I hardly know . . . look at this statue . . . it's of the wife when she was young.

JOHANSSON: Oh, good Lord! Is this the Mummy?

BENGTSSON: Yes. Pathetic, isn't it? But this woman has been endowed with some qualities usually associated with the chattering bird, either through her power of imagination or something else . . . and she can't stand cripples or people who are ill . . . she can't stand her own daughter because she's sick . . .

JOHANSSON: Is the young lady sick?

BENGTSSON: Didn't you know?

JOHANSSON: No! And who is the colonel?

BENGTSSON: You'll see.

JOHANSSON: *(Looks at the statue.)* It's terrible to think . . . how old is the wife now?

BENGTSSON: Nobody knows, but people say that when she was thirty-five she looked like nineteen and she persuaded the colonel that she was . . . Here in this house . . . do you know what that black Japanese screen is for, the one beside the chaise-longue? It's called the death screen and it's taken out when someone is about to die, just like they do in the hospitals . . .

JOHANSSON: What a terrible house . . . and the student pined for this place as if it were paradise . . .

BENGTSSON: Which student? Oh, him! The one who is coming here tonight . . . the colonel and the young lady met him at the opera and they were both charmed by him . . . hm! But now it's my turn to ask questions: Who is your employer? The director in the wheel-chair . . .?

JOHANSSON: Yes, yes. Is he coming here too?

BENGTSSON: Well, he's not invited.

JOHANSSON: He'll come uninvited, if necessary . . .

>*The Old Man visible in the hall with his overcoat, top hat and crutches, he sneaks forward, listening.*

BENGTSSON: He's a real fiend, isn't he?

JOHANSSON: Fully-fledged.

BENGTSSON: He looks like the devil himself.

JOHANSSON: And he's supposed to be a bit of a magician too . . . they say he can walk through locked doors . . .

OLD MAN: *(Comes forward, pulls Johansson's ear.)* Thief! Watch
              out! *(To Bengtsson.)* Notify the colonel about my
              presence!

BENGTSSON: But they're expecting visitors now . . .

OLD MAN: I know. But my visit is almost expected, if not exactly
              longed for . . .

BENGTSSON: I see. What was the name again? Mr Hummel?

OLD MAN: That's right. *(Bengtsson walks through the hall to the
              green room, closing the door behind him. Old Man to
              Johansson:)* Get out of the way! *(Johansson hesitates.)*
              Get out! *(Johansson retreats into the hall. Old Man views
              the room, stops in front of the statue, greatly surprised.)*
              Amalia! It's her! Her! *(He walks around in the room,
              touches a few things, arranges his wig in front of the
              mirror; returns to the statue.)*

THE MUMMY: *(From inside the wardrobe.)* Prrretty Polly!

OLD MAN: *(Shocked)* What was that? Is there a parrot in the
              room? I can't see one.

THE MUMMY: Is Jacob there?

OLD MAN: It must be a poltergeist.

THE MUMMY: Jacob!

OLD MAN: It's eerie. So this is the kind of secret they keep in this
              house. *(He looks at a picture, his back to the wardrobe.)*
              There he is. It's him.

MUMMY: *(Enters, behind the Old Man, tugs at his wig.)* Crrr . . .
              is it . . . Crrr?

OLD MAN: *(Reacts)* Jesus Christ. Who is it?

MUMMY: *(In a human voice.)* Is it Jacob?

OLD MAN: Yes, my name is Jacob, as a matter of fact.

MUMMY: *(In an affected voice.)* And my name is Amalia.

OLD MAN: Oh no, no, no . . . Good Lord . . .

MUMMY: Oh dear, look at me! What a mess! Goodness me,
              compared to the way I used to look! Life is a learning
              process – I live in the wardrobe most of the time, so I

don't have to see . . . so I don't have to be seen . . .
But Jacob, what are you looking for here?

OLD MAN: My child! Our child!

MUMMY: She is sitting over there!

OLD MAN: Where?

MUMMY: There, in the hyacinth room.

OLD MAN: *(Looking at the young lady.)* Yes, it's her alright. *(Pause)* What does her father say, I mean the colonel . . . your husband?

MUMMY: Once when I was angry with him I told him everything . . .

OLD MAN: And . . .?

MUMMY: He didn't believe me, he just said: "That's what all wives say when they want to kill their husbands." It was a frightful crime anyway. His whole life has been a lie, his family name has been sullied; I read the book on peerage sometimes and then I think: She is walking around with a false birth certificate like a simple maid and the punishment for that is prison.

OLD MAN: She's not the only one doing that; I seem to remember that you had the wrong date of birth too . . .

MUMMY: It was my mother who told me to . . . it's not my fault. But you were the one most to blame for our crime . . .

OLD MAN: No, it was your husband who brought it about when he took my fiancée away from me. I was born that way . . . I could never forgive anyone until I'd punished him, I regarded it as a duty . . . I still do.

MUMMY: What are you looking for in this house? What do you want? How did you get in? Is it about my daughter? If you touch her you'll die.

OLD MAN: I don't want to do her any harm.

MUMMY: You must leave her father alone.

OLD MAN: No.

MUMMY: Then you must die; in this room; behind this screen . . .

OLD MAN: Be that as it may . . . but once I've got my teeth in, I can't let go.

MUMMY: You want to marry her off to that student . . . why? He's a nobody and he hasn't got a penny.

OLD MAN: I'll make him rich.

MUMMY: Are you invited here this evening?

OLD MAN: No, but I'm going to invite myself to the ghost supper.

MUMMY: Do you know who is coming?

OLD MAN: Not quite.

MUMMY: Baron so-and-so . . . who lives on the floor above and whose father-in-law was buried today . . .

OLD MAN: The one who is getting a divorce in order to marry the concierge's daughter . . . the one who was your lover once.

MUMMY: And your ex-fiancée is coming too . . . the woman who was later seduced by my husband . . .

OLD MAN: A nice little gathering . . .

MUMMY: God, if only we could die. If we could die.

OLD MAN: Why do you keep seeing these people if you feel like this?

MUMMY: Crimes and secrets . . . and feelings of guilt bind us together. We have broken up and parted company many many times, but sooner or later we've been drawn together again . . .

OLD MAN: I think the colonel is coming now . . .

MUMMY: Then I'll go and join Adèle . . . *(Pause)* Jacob, think of what you're doing. Leave him alone! *(Pause. She leaves.)*

COLONEL: *(Enters, cold, reserved.)* Please, take a seat. *(The Old Man sits down slowly. Pause. Colonel stares at him.)* Is it you who wrote this letter, sir?

OLD MAN: Yes.

COLONEL: And your name is Hummel?

OLD MAN: Yes.

COLONEL: Now that I know that it's you who paid off my debts it seems that I'm in your hands, sir. What do you want me to do?

OLD MAN: I want to be repaid, in one way or another.

COLONEL: In what way?

OLD MAN: A very simple way, but don't let's talk about money now, just allow me to be your guest.

COLONEL: If that's all . . .

OLD MAN: Thank you.

COLONEL: And then what?

OLD MAN: Dismiss Bengtsson.

COLONEL: Why should I do that? My loyal servant who's been with me for a whole generation – who's been awarded the country's greatest decoration for faithful service – why should I do that?

OLD MAN: All these noble qualities . . . that's just how he appears in your imagination. He's not the man he appears to be, you know.

COLONEL: Who is?

OLD MAN: True! But Bengtsson must go.

COLONEL: Do you want to rule in my house?

OLD MAN: Yes, because it's all mine now: the furniture, the curtains, the china and linen . . . etcetera.

COLONEL: What . . . etcetera?

OLD MAN: Everything. Everything you see around you is mine. Yes, mine.

COLONEL: Alright, so it's yours. But the family crest and my good name remains mine.

OLD MAN: No, not even that. *(Pause)* You're not a nobleman.

COLONEL: How dare you?

OLD MAN: *(Produces a piece of paper.)* If you read this extract from the book of heraldry you'll see that the family whose

name you carry has been extinct for over a hundred
years.

COLONEL: *(Reads)* I had heard rumours to that effect, but I got
the name after my father . . . *(Reads)* It's true, you're
right . . . I'm not a nobleman. Not even that. I shall
remove my signet ring. It's true, it belongs to you.
Here you are!

OLD MAN: *(Puts the ring in his pocket.)* Now, let's carry on. You're
not a colonel either.

COLONEL: Aren't I?

OLD MAN: No! You've served as a colonel in . . . in the American
Voluntary Forces but after the Cuban war . . . and the
reorganisation of the army, all previous titles were
withdrawn . . .

COLONEL: Is that true?

OLD MAN: *(With a gesture towards his pocket.)* Do you want to read
this?

COLONEL: No, there's no need. Who do you think you are to strip
me in this way?

OLD MAN: We shall see. But as far as stripping is concerned, do
you know who you are?

COLONEL: You ought to be ashamed of yourself.

OLD MAN: Go on, take your wig off and look yourself in the
mirror, and take the dentures out too while you're at it
and shave off your moustache, let Bengtsson loosen
your iron corset and we'll see if the man-servant XYZ
recognizes himself; the man who begged food from a
certain kitchen quarters . . . *(The Colonel reaches for a
bell on the table. Old Man prevents him.)* Don't touch
the bell, don't call Bengtsson because then I'll have
him arrested. Here are the guests now, keep calm and
we shall go on playing our old parts.

COLONEL: Who are you? I recognize your eyes and your voice . . .

OLD MAN: Don't think about that now, just keep quiet and do as I
tell you.

STUDENT: *(Enters, bows in the direction of the Colonel.)* Sir!

COLONEL: Welcome to my house, young man. After your noble conduct at the place of the terrible accident your name is on everybody's lips and I consider it an honour to welcome you to my home . . .

STUDENT: Sir, my humble birth . . . your glorious and noble name . . .

COLONEL: May I introduce Mr Arkenholz, undergraduate, Mr Hummel managing director. Would you care to go in and meet the ladies while I finish my conversation with Mr Hummel . . . *(The Student is shown into the hyacinth room where he remains visible while talking shyly to the young lady.)* A superb young man, with musical talent, he sings, writes poetry . . . if he were a nobleman and an equal I wouldn't mind . . . well . . .

OLD MAN: What?

COLONEL: My daughter . . .

OLD MAN: Your daughter? By the way, why does she spend all her time in there?

COLONEL: She insists on staying in the hyacinth room when she is not outdoors. It is one of those things with her . . . Here comes Miss Beate von Holsteinkrona . . . a charming woman . . . a member of the Society of Single Women of Noble Birth . . . with an annuity suitably large enough for her class and circumstances . . .

OLD MAN: *(To himself.)* My fiancée.

The Fiancée, white-haired, looks crazed.

COLONEL: Miss Holsteinkrona . . . Mr Hummel. *(The Fiancée curtseys and sits down. The Nobleman enters, looking secretive; dressed in mourning, sits down.)* Baron Skansborg . . .

OLD MAN: *(Aside, without getting up.)* I think it's the jewel thief . . . *(To the Colonel.)* Let the mummy join us and then we're all gathered . . .

COLONEL: *(In the doorway to the hyacinth room.)* Polly!

MUMMY: *(Enters)* Crrr . . .

COLONEL: Are we going to let the young people in too?

OLD MAN: No, not the young people. We'll leave them alone . . .

Everybody is now seated in a circle. Nobody speaks.

COLONEL: Can we bring the tea in now?

OLD MAN: What's the point? Nobody likes tea anyway so why pretend and sit here like hypocrites?

Pause.

COLONEL: Shall we have a conversation then?

OLD MAN: *(Slowly and with many pauses.)* You mean talk about the weather . . . which we all know . . . or ask each other how we are, which we know . . . no, I prefer the silence, so one can hear one's thoughts and visualize the past; silence cannot conceal anything . . . unlike words. I read somewhere the other day that different languages came about as a way of hiding one tribe's secrets from another; languages are like codes . . . if you find the key you can understand all the languages in the world; but that doesn't prevent you from deciphering the secrets without a key, especially in cases where paternity needs to be proved . . . but proof before a court of justice is another matter, of course; two false witnesses are sufficient to prove a person's guilt or innocence as long as they agree . . . but the kind of expeditions I'm referring to don't allow any witnesses to be present in the act . . . nature has endowed man with a sense of modesty which endeavours to conceal that which should be concealed; however, we tend to slide into situations unwittingly and sometimes opportunities arise when the innermost secrets have to be revealed . . . when the mask has to be pulled from the deceiver . . . when the villain is revealed . . . *(Pause, everybody looks at each other in silence.)* It suddenly became very quiet. *(Long silence.)* Here for instance, in this respectable house, in this lovely home, where beauty, culture and wealth have been united . . . *(Long silence.)* All of us who are gathered here know who we are . . . don't we? I don't need to tell you . . . and you all know me even though you feign ignorance . . . in there is my daughter, yes, my daughter . . . you know that too . . . She'd lost her desire to live, without knowing why . . . she faded away in this air which

breathed crime, deception and all kinds of falsehood
. . . so I found her a friend in whose company she
could perceive the glow and warmth of a noble deed
. . . *(Long silence.)* That was my mission in this house;
to clear away the weeds, to reveal the crimes, settle the
accounts to give the young people a fresh start in this
house . . . which I've now given to them. *(Long silence.)*
You can all leave now . . . in an orderly fashion, please.
The one who stays behind will be arrested. *(Long
silence.)* Can you hear the clock ticking, it sounds like
the death-watch beetle? Can you hear what she says?
"Time passes, time passes . . ." In a little while when
the clock strikes, your time is up . . . then you can go
but not before. But before she strikes she wags her
finger. Listen. Now she comes with a warning: "The
clock can strike." I too can strike . . . *(He strikes his
stick on the table.)* Did you hear?

> Silence.

MUMMY: *(Walks up to the clock and stops in front of it, then
seriously and clearly.)* But I can stop time in its course
. . . I can abolish the past, obliterate the events that
have already taken place, not with bribes, not with
threats – but through suffering and regrets . . . *(Walks
up to the Old Man.)* We're poor wretches and we know
it, we've sinned like everyone else, we're not what we
seem . . . deep down we're better than ourselves
because we dislike our wrong-doings; but how can you,
Jacob Hummel, with your false name sit there in
judgement . . . that just shows that you're worse than
the rest of us. You're not the one you appear to be
either. You're a thief . . . you stole me once with false
promises and you killed the consul who was buried
here today, you strangled him with debit notes; you've
stolen the student by tying him with a fictitious debt
that his father was supposed to have . . . but he never
owed you an öre . . . *(The Old Man has tried to get up
and speak but has fallen back into his chair and shrunk;
he shrinks more and more during the following.)* But
there's a dark secret in your life too which I'm not
quite sure about but I think Bengtsson can fill us in.
(Rings the bell on the table.)

OLD MAN: No, not Bengtsson. Not him!

MUMMY: I see, so he does know. *(Rings the bell again. We can
              now see the little Milkmaid in the hallway but she is
              invisible to everybody but the Old Man who looks
              frightened; the girl disappears as Bengtsson enters.)* Do
              you know this gentleman, Bengtsson?

BENGTSSON: Yes, I know him and he knows me too. Life vacillates
              as we all know . . . I've been in his service and he's
              been in mine too. He came begging for food in my
              kitchen for two whole years and because he had to
              leave at three o'clock the dinner had to be ready at two,
              and the rest of the household had to eat heated up food
              after that ox . . . but he drank the goodness out of the
              meat juices as well so they had to be diluted after he'd
              had his fill . . . he sat there like a vampire and sucked
              all the life-blood out of the house so we became like
              skeletons and he almost got us into prison when we
              accused the cook of being a thief. Later on, I came
              across this man in Hamburg, using an assumed name.
              Then he was a usurer, a blood-sucker; but over there
              he was also accused of luring a young girl onto the ice
              in order to drown her. She'd witnessed a crime that
              he'd committed and he was afraid of being discovered
              . . .

MUMMY: *(Touches the Old Man's face with her hand.)* That man
              is you! Give us the debit notes and the will now.
              *(Johansson visible in the hallway, looking at the scene with
              great interest now that he is released from his slavery. The
              Old Man produces a pile of papers and throws them on
              the table. Mummy strokes the Old Man's back.)* Birdie
              . . . Jacob are you there?

OLD MAN: *(Imitating a parrot.)* Jacob's here. Cacadora! Dora!

MUMMY: Can the clock strike?

OLD MAN: *(Clucking)* The clock can strike. *(Imitates a cuckoo
              clock.)* Cuckoo, cuckoo, cuckoo . . .

MUMMY: *(Opens the door to the wardrobe.)* Now the time's come.
              Get up and go into the wardrobe where I've spent
              twenty years crying about our indiscretion. There is a
              piece of string in there which will remind you of the
              one you strangled the consul with upstairs . . . and the
              one you meant to strangle your benefactor with. In you

go now! *(The Old Man goes into the wardrobe. Mummy closes the door behind him.)* Bengtsson! Put the screen up, please! The death screen! *(Bengtsson puts the screen in front of the door.)* It is done. God preserve his soul.

ALL: Amen.

Long silence.

In the hyacinth room the Young Lady is sitting beside a harp. She is accompanying the Student who is reciting.

RECITATION:
(Preceded by a prelude.)
I saw the sun, and it was like
seeing the Hidden One;
each person reaps what he has sown,
blessed are those who take delight in virtue.
After striking out in wrath,
do not take vengeance;
give solace where you've caused distress;
virtue hath her own rewards.
He who does no wrong has naught to fear;
it is good to be in a state of grace.

SCENE THREE

A somewhat bizarre room with oriental motifs. Hyacinths of all colours everywhere. On the stove there is a large bust of Buddha with a big rotating disc on his lap and from that springs a stalk of a shallot bulb, carrying a spherical flower-head with white stamens.

At the back, on the right, a door leading to the round drawing-room where the Colonel and the Mummy are sitting immobile and silent; a part of the death screen is also visible; to the left, a door leading to the kitchen.

The Student and the Young Lady (Adèle) are beside the table; she by her harp, he standing.

YOUNG LADY: Please, sing for my flowers now.

STUDENT: Is this the flower of your soul?

YOUNG LADY: It's my only one. Do you love hyacinths?

STUDENT: I love them more than any other flower . . . their
             virginal shape . . . that rises from the ground, slim and
             straight, rests on the water and lowers its white pure
             roots in the colourless fluid; I love its colours; the
             snow-white innocence, the lovely honey-colour, the
             young pink, the ripe red, but above all the blue one,
             the dewy-blue, deep-eyed, faithful one; I love them all,
             more than gold and pearls, I've loved them ever since I
             was a child, I've admired them because of the beautiful
             qualities they possess . . . qualities that I lack . . . but
             . . .

YOUNG LADY: What?

STUDENT: My love is unrequited, the pretty flowers hate me . . .

YOUNG LADY: How?

STUDENT: Their smell, strong and purified by the first spring
             breeze that sweeps across the melting snow . . . this
             smell confuses me, drugs me, dazzles me, pushes me
             out of the room, shoots at me with poisonous arrows
             which make my heart sad and my head hot. Don't you
             know that fairy tale about the flower?

YOUNG LADY: Tell me!

STUDENT: But first, let's try and find out the meaning. The round
             disc represents the earth which rests on the water or
             lies in the soil, here the stalk shoots up, straight as the
             axis of the world and at the top end are the six-pronged
             star-shaped flowers.

YOUNG LADY: Above the earth . . . the stars. Oh, it's grand, where did
             you learn that, how did you see that?

STUDENT: Let me think. In your eyes. It's an image of Cosmos
             . . . that's why Buddha is sitting there with the rotating
             earth on his lap, with his roving eye so he can see it
             grow and rise and transform itself into a heaven. The
             poor earth is going to turn into heaven. That's what
             Buddha is waiting for.

YOUNG LADY: Now I can see . . . doesn't the snowdrop also have six
             stamens like the hyacinth?

STUDENT: You said it! The snow flowers are falling stars . . .

YOUNG LADY: And the snowdrop is a snow star . . . grown out of the snow.

STUDENT: But Sirius, the biggest and most beautiful of all the stars in the firmament, is the narcissus edged with crimson and yellow and with its six white stamens . . .

YOUNG LADY: Have you seen the shallot bulb in bloom?

STUDENT: Yes, of course I have. It carries its flowers in a ball, a globe which resembles the heavenly orb strewn with white stars . . .

YOUNG LADY: Yes, it is truly splendid. Whose idea was it?

STUDENT: Yours!

YOUNG LADY: No, yours!

STUDENT: Ours! We've given birth to something together, we're married . . .

YOUNG LADY: Not yet . . .

STUDENT: What remains to be done?

YOUNG LADY: First there is the long wait, the trials . . . the forbearance.

STUDENT: Well, try me! *(Pause)* Tell me! Why do your parents sit there so silent . . . without uttering a word?

YOUNG LADY: Because they have nothing to say to each other, because the one doesn't believe what the other one is saying. My father's explained it like this: What's the point of speaking, we can't pull wool over each other's eyes, anyway.

STUDENT: It sounds terrible . . .

YOUNG LADY: Here comes the cook . . . look at her, look how big and fat she is . . .

STUDENT: What does she want?

YOUNG LADY: She wants to ask me about the dinner, I'm in charge of the household while my mother is ill, you see . . .

STUDENT: Do we have to be involved with the kitchen?

YOUNG LADY: We must eat, after all. Look at the cook, I can't see her . . .

STUDENT: Who is that giant of a woman?

YOUNG LADY: She belongs to a family of vampires, the Hummels, she
            eats us all up . . .

STUDENT: Why don't you get rid of her?

YOUNG LADY: She won't leave. We can't touch her, we've got her for
            our sins . . . can't you see that we're languishing away,
            wasting away . . .

STUDENT: Don't you get anything to eat then?

YOUNG LADY: Oh yes, she gives us a lot to eat, but all the nutrition is
            gone . . . She boils the goodness out of the meat and
            gives us the sinews and water while she drinks the
            stock; and when we have a joint she'll boil it first, then
            she'll eat the sauce, drink the juices; everything she
            touches loses its strength, it's as if she were sucking it
            out with her eyes; we get the dregs when she's had her
            coffee, she drinks up the wine and fills the bottles with
            water . . .

STUDENT: Get rid of her!

YOUNG LADY: We can't.

STUDENT: Why?

YOUNG LADY: We don't know. She won't go. Nobody can touch her –
            she's made us all powerless.

STUDENT: Will you let me get rid of her?

YOUNG LADY: No! Things must remain as they are. Here she is now.
            She'll ask what I want for dinner, I'll tell her this and
            that; she'll raise objections and in the end she'll do as
            she likes, anyway.

STUDENT: Why not let her decide then?

YOUNG LADY: She doesn't want to.

STUDENT: It's a strange house. There seems no way out.

YOUNG LADY: No. She's turned away now that she's seen you.

COOK: (In the doorway.) No, that wasn't the reason. (Grins,
            showing her teeth.)

STUDENT: Out, woman.

COOK: When it suits me, yes. *(Pause)* Now I'll go. *(Disappears)*

YOUNG LADY:Don't rush things. Try to be patient; she was sent to us as a trial. We have a housemaid too . . . whom we have to clean up after.

STUDENT: I feel I'm sinking. *Cor in aethere.* Time for a song.

YOUNG LADY:Wait.

STUDENT: A song!

YOUNG LADY:Don't get carried away! This is called the room of trials – it's pretty to look at but it's full of defects . . .

STUDENT: Incredible; but you have to overlook them. It's attractive but a little cold. Why don't you heat it?

YOUNG LADY:Because the stove always smokes.

STUDENT: Can't you get a chimney-sweep?

YOUNG LADY:It doesn't help. Do you see the desk over there?

STUDENT: Very beautiful.

YOUNG LADY:But it's uneven; every day I put a piece of cork under one of its legs but the housemaid removes it when she sweeps the floor and I have to cut out a new one. Every morning the whole pen is covered with ink and so is all the writing material. I have to wash everything after her, every blessed day. *(Pause)* What's the worst thing you can think of?

STUDENT: Counting the laundry.

YOUNG LADY:That's my job. *(Sighs)*

STUDENT: And what else?

YOUNG LADY:To be disturbed in the middle of the night because the maid has forgotten to put the catch on the window, so I have to get up and do it.

STUDENT: What else?

YOUNG LADY:To climb a ladder and fix the damper string after the maid has pulled it off.

STUDENT: And what else?

YOUNG LADY: To sweep after her, to dust after her, to make up a fire in the stove after her; she just puts the logs there. To watch the damper, dry the glasses, re-lay the table, uncork the bottles, open the windows to air the apartment, re-make my bed, clean the water carafe when it's green with algae, buy matches and soap . . . because they're always missing, dry the lamp and cut the wicks to stop the lamps from going out or filling the room with smoke. When we have visitors I have to refill the lamps myself . . .

STUDENT: A song!

YOUNG LADY: Wait! First the labours . . . the tasks we have to perform to keep the unclean things in life at a distance.

STUDENT: But you're wealthy, you have two servants.

YOUNG LADY: It doesn't help. Even if we had three . . . Life is difficult and I'm so tired sometimes . . . just imagine having a nursery as well!

STUDENT: The greatest of joys . . .

YOUNG LADY: The most expensive . . . Is life worth all that trouble?

STUDENT: It depends how you expect to be rewarded for your pains . . . I wouldn't stop at anything to win your hand.

YOUNG LADY: Don't speak like that. I can never be yours.

STUDENT: Why?

YOUNG LADY: You mustn't ask me that.

Pause.

STUDENT: You dropped your bracelet through the window . . .

YOUNG LADY: Because my wrist has become so thin . . . *(Pause. The Cook can be seen with a Japanese bottle in her hand.)* It's she who nibbles away at me . . . and at all of us.

STUDENT: What has she got in her hand?

YOUNG LADY: The colouring bottle with the scorpion letters. It is the soy sauce which turns water into bouillon, which replaces the sauce, which she cooks the cabbage in and makes turtle soup of.

STUDENT: Out!

COOK: You suck the goodness out of us and we out of you; we take the blood and give you the water – with colouring. It's colouring. I'm going now, but I'll stay anyway, as long as I want to. *(Leaves)*

STUDENT: Why is Bengtsson wearing a medal?

YOUNG LADY: It's for all his great merits.

STUDENT: Has he no faults?

YOUNG LADY: Yes, lots but you don't get decorated for those. *(They smile.)*

STUDENT: You have a lot of secrets in this house . . .

YOUNG LADY: Like everyone else, let us keep ours.

              Pause.

STUDENT: Do you love frankness?

YOUNG LADY: In moderation.

STUDENT: Sometimes I get such an urge to speak my mind, but I know that the world would collapse if everyone was honest all the time. *(Pause)* I went to a funeral the other day . . . in the church . . . it was very solemn and beautiful.

YOUNG LADY: Mr Hummel's?

STUDENT: My false benefactor's, yes. At his coffin stood an elderly friend of the deceased and he carried the staff; I was especially impressed by the priest's dignity and moving words. Yes, we cried, we all cried. Afterwards we went to an inn . . . there I learnt that the man who led the funeral procession had been in love with the son of the deceased . . . *(Young Lady looks at him to work out the meaning of this.)* And I found out that the dead man had borrowed money from his son's admirer . . . *(Pause)* The day afterwards, the priest was arrested for embezzling the church funds. Pretty story, isn't it?

YOUNG LADY: Ugh!

              Pause.

STUDENT: Do you know what I think about you?

YOUNG LADY: Don't tell me, because then I'll die.

STUDENT: I must, or I'll die.

YOUNG LADY: At the asylum they say that everything you think . . .

STUDENT: That's right. My father ended up in a lunatic asylum
            . . .

YOUNG LADY: Was he ill?

STUDENT: No, he wasn't ill, but he was mad. His madness broke
            out like this . . . he was surrounded by a group of
            people whom for the sake of brevity he called friends;
            they were a bunch of good-for-nothings, of course, like
            most people. But he had to have some social life . . . he
            didn't like being on his own. Anyway, one doesn't tell
            people to their face what one thinks of them, not
            normally anyway and nor did he. He knew what a
            bunch of hypocrites they were, he knew about their
            disloyality . . . but he was a wise man and well brought
            up so he was always polite. But one day he gave a big
            party – it was in the evening . . . he was tired after a
            day's work and because of the strain of keeping quiet
            on the one hand and engaging in small talk on the
            other . . . *(Young Lady looks shocked.)* Anyway, he
            tapped the table and asked for silence, lifted his glass to
            make a speech . . . then all his inhibitions went and in
            a long speech he stripped the whole party, one after the
            other, told them how false they were. And when he'd
            finished he sat down in the middle of the table,
            exhausted, and asked them to go to hell.

YOUNG LADY: Oh!

STUDENT: I was there and I'll never forget what happened
            afterwards. Father and mother had a fight, the guests
            rushed towards the door . . . and father was taken to
            the madhouse where he died. *(Pause)* If you keep silent
            for too long, stagnant water collects and rots inside you
            and that's how it is in this house too. There is
            something rotten here! The first time I saw you going
            in here I thought it was paradise . . . I used to stand
            here on Sunday mornings and look in through the
            window. I saw a colonel who wasn't a colonel, I had a
            noble benefactor who was a gangster and hanged

himself; I saw a mummy who wasn't a mummy and a
virgin . . . by the way where is virginity? Where is
beauty? In nature and in my head when it is dressed in
its Sunday best. Where is honour and faith? In fairy
tales and at children's shows. Where is the thing that
holds what it promises? In my imagination. Your
flowers have poisoned me and I've returned the poison
to you – I asked you to be my wife, we made up poems
together, sang and played and then the cook turned up
. . . *Sursum Corda*! Try once more to strike divine
sparks from the golden harp . . . try, I ask you, I
implore you on my knees . . . Alright then, I'll do it
myself. *(Takes the harp but the strings don't give off any
sound.)* It's deaf and dumb. Isn't it sad that the most
beautiful flowers are so poisonous, are the most
poisonous ones, the whole creation and life itself is
cursed . . . Why didn't you want to be my bride?
Because you're ill at the very source of life . . . now I
can feel how the vampire in the kitchen is beginning to
suck me, I think it's a demon giving suck to children,
it's always in the kitchen where the children are
pinched in the bud, unless it's in the bedroom of
course . . . there are poisons which impair the sight and
poisons which open your eyes. I must be born with the
latter because I cannot interpret the ugly as beautiful or
call the bad good. I can't! Jesus Christ descended into
hell, that was his journey on earth, to the mad-house,
the house of correction, the mortuary that is earth; and
the madmen killed him when he wanted to release
them, but the gangster was set free, the gangster always
has the people's sympathy. Pity, pity on us all. Saviour
of the world, deliver us, we're perishing!

*The Young Lady has collapsed, looks lifeless, rings her
bell. Bengtsson enters.*

YOUNG LADY: Bring me the screen. Quickly . . . I'm dying.

*Bengtsson returns with the screen which he unfolds and
puts in front of the Young Lady.*

STUDENT: The Saviour is coming. Welcome, you pale, meek . . .
go to sleep, my beautiful, innocent creature, who
suffers even though you're without guilt . . . sleep
without dreams and when you wake up again . . . may

you be greeted by a sun which doesn't burn, in a home
without dust, with relatives without shame, by a love
without flaws. You wise, meek Buddha who sit there
waiting for a heaven to take shape on earth . . . help us
to endure our hardships, make our wishes pure so that
our hopes may not be frustrated. *(The harp's strings are
giving off a sound and the room is filled with a strong
light.)*
I saw the sun and it was like
seeing the Hidden One;
each person reaps what he has sown,
blessed are those who take delight in virtue.
After striking out in wrath,
do not take vengeance;
give solace where you've caused distress;
virtue hath her own rewards.
He who does no wrong has naught to fear;
it is good to be in a state of grace.
(A moaning noise can be heard behind the screen.)
You poor little child, child of this world of delusions,
guilt, suffering and death; the world of constant
changes, disappointments and pain. May the Lord in
Heaven bless you on your journey . . .

> *The room disappears. Boecklin's 'Toten-insel' appears
> as backcloth; faint music, quiet and pleasingly sad, can
> be heard from the 'Toten-insel'.*

THE END

Opus 4
THE PELICAN

CHARACTERS

THE MOTHER   (Elise, widow)

THE SON   (Fredrik, law student)

THE DAUGHTER   (Gerda)

THE SON-IN-LAW   (Axel, married to Gerda)

MARGRET   (Servant)

SCENE ONE

A drawing-room; at the back a door leading to the dining-room; we can glimpse a balcony door to the right. A secretaire, a desk, a chaise-longue with a scarlet cover; a rocking chair.

The Mother enters, dressed in mourning. She sits down in an armchair. Now and then she listens and looks worried. Off-stage, Chopin's "Fantasie Impromptu Oeuvre Posthume Op. 66" is being played.

Margret, the cook, enters from the back.

THE
MOTHER :   Close the door, please.

MARGRET :   Are you on your own, madam?

THE
MOTHER :   Close the door, please. *(Short pause.)* Who is that playing?

MARGRET :   It's a terrible night, what with a howling wind and pouring rain . . .

THE
MOTHER :   Close the door, please, that smell of carbolic acid and fir twigs reek of death . . .

MARGRET :   I know, madam, that's why I suggested you took your poor late husband straight to the chapel . . .

THE
MOTHER :   But the children insisted on having the funeral service at home . . .

MARGRET :   Why do you stay on here, madam, why don't you move away?

THE
MOTHER :   The landlord won't let us leave, we can't move . . . *(Pause)* Why did you take the cover off the red chaise-longue?

MARGRET :   It needed to be washed. *(Pause)* You know . . . well, the master breathed his last on that very sofa . . . why don't you have it removed . . .

THE
MOTHER: I'm not allowed to touch anything before the estate
              inventory has been completed . . . that's why I'm
              incarcerated here . . . and I can't go into the other
              rooms . . .

MARGRET: Why is that?

THE
MOTHER: Memories . . . all the unpleasant things that have taken
              place in there . . . and that dreadful smell . . . Is that
              my son playing?

MARGRET: Yes, he doesn't like being in here . . . makes him
              restless; and he's always hungry, says he's never had
              enough to eat . . .

THE
MOTHER: He's been a sickly child since birth . . .

MARGRET: Bottle-fed babies need lots of solids once they are
              weaned . . .

THE
MOTHER: (Sharply) What do you mean? Has he been wanting for
              anything?

MARGRET: Not exactly, but all the same . . . you shouldn't have
              bought the cheapest and worst quality food all the time,
              madam . . . and sending the children off to school on a
              breakfast consisting of chicory and a bread-roll . . . it's
              not right, madam . . .

THE
MOTHER: My children have never complained of the food . . .

MARGRET: Haven't they? Not to you perhaps, because they didn't
              dare, but when they were growing up they used to
              come and see me in the kitchen . . .

THE
MOTHER: We've always been hard up . . .

MARGRET: Oh no, that's not true . . . I read in the paper that your
              late husband had a taxable income of 20,000 *kronor* . . .

THE
MOTHER: It didn't go very far!

MARGRET: Oh yes. Oh yes . . . but they are delicate children . . . Miss Gerda . . . I mean young Mrs Gerda isn't full-grown yet even though she is over twenty . . .

THE
MOTHER: What are you saying?

MARGRET: Never mind. *(Pause)* Shall I light a fire for you, madam? It's cold in here.

THE
MOTHER: No thank you. We can't afford to burn up our money . . .

MARGRET: But young Fredrik is always shivering; he has to go for a walk or play the piano to keep warm . . .

THE
MOTHER: He's always been a cold boy . . .

MARGRET: And why do you think that is?

THE
MOTHER: Watch your tongue, Margret . . . *(Pause)* Is someone walking about out there?

MARGRET: No, there's no one walking about . . .

THE
MOTHER: Do you think I'm afraid of ghosts?

MARGRET: I don't know. How should I know? One thing's for certain, I'm not staying here for much longer . . . I came here as if doomed to look after the children once . . . and when I saw how the servants were maltreated, I wanted to leave but I couldn't . . . or I wasn't allowed to . . . Now when Miss Gerda is married I feel my mission is completed, soon I shall be released again . . . but not quite yet . . .

THE
MOTHER: I don't understand a word you're saying . . . everybody knows how much I've sacrificed for my children, how I've looked after my house and done my duty . . . you're the only one accusing me, but I don't care. You're free to leave whenever you want to. I don't intend to have any more servants once the young couple move into this apartment . . .

MARGRET: I hope they'll look after you well, madam . . . children aren't grateful by nature, and mothers-in-law aren't very popular unless they bring money with them . . .

THE
MOTHER: Don't worry about me . . . I shall pay for my board and help around in the house . . . besides, my son-in-law is different . . .

MARGRET: Is he?

THE
MOTHER: Yes, he is. He doesn't treat me like a mother-in-law, more like a sister, or friend even . . . *(Margret makes a face.)* I know what that's supposed to mean. I'm fond of my son-in-law, yes, but there's nothing wrong in that. He deserves it . . . my husband didn't like him, he was envious . . . jealous even, yes, he actually did me the honour of being jealous . . . despite my mature age . . . did you say something?

MARGRET: No, I didn't say anything . . . but I thought I heard someone coming. It's young Fredrik, I can tell by his cough. Shall I light a fire?

THE
MOTHER: There's no need.

MARGRET: Madam! I've been starving and freezing in this house, but I've put up with it. Now all I ask for is a bed, a proper bed please . . . I'm old and tired . . .

THE
MOTHER: It's hardly worth it now that you're about to leave . . .

MARGRET: That's true. I forgot. But for the sake of family honour please burn my old bed clothes which have been used on death beds . . . I don't want you to be put to shame by the person who comes after me . . . if someone does, that is.

THE
MOTHER: We're not having anyone after you.

MARGRET: But if you should change your mind, I'm sure she won't stay . . . I've seen fifty housemaids come and go in this house . . .

THE
MOTHER: It's because they were bad people, you all are . . .

MARGRET: Thank you very much. *(Short pause.)* Well . . . now it's your turn. It will always be someone's turn. Sooner or later.

THE
MOTHER: Have you finished soon?

MARGRET: Yes, soon, very soon. Sooner than you think. *(Leaves)*

The Son enters with a book, coughing. He's got a slight stutter.

THE
MOTHER: Shut the door after you, please.

THE SON: Why?

THE
MOTHER: Is that a way to answer your mother? What do you want?

THE SON: May I sit down here and read. It's so cold in my room.

THE
MOTHER: You're always cold, aren't you?

THE SON: When you sit still you feel the cold more. *(Pause. He pretends to read.)* Is the estate inventory finished yet?

THE
MOTHER: Why do you ask? Can't you allow a proper period of mourning first? Don't you miss your father?

THE SON: Yes, but he's probably better off where he is . . . and I don't begrudge him some peace and quiet . . . he's finally found peace. But that doesn't stop me from finding out about my position . . . I want to know if I can finish my studies without borrowing any money . . .

THE
MOTHER: Your father didn't leave anything, you know that, some debts, that's all . . .

THE SON: But isn't the business worth something?

THE
MOTHER: You can't call it a business when there's no stock, no goods.

THE SON: *(Pauses first.)* But the firm, the name, the customers . . .

THE
MOTHER: One can't sell customers . . .

Pause.

THE SON: I've heard that it's possible.

THE
MOTHER: Have you been to see a lawyer? *(Pause)* Is that the way you grieve for your father?

THE SON: No, not like that. But you've got to keep things separate. Where is Gerda and her husband?

THE
MOTHER: They came back from their honeymoon this morning and they're staying in a boarding-house at the moment.

THE SON: That means they'll have enough to eat at least.

THE
MOTHER: Always talking about food! Have you got any complaints about my food?

THE SON: Not exactly.

THE
MOTHER: But tell me something . . . towards the end . . . you know, when I was living on my own for a while, and you and father used to go for walks . . . did he ever talk about his business then?

THE SON: *(Engrossed in his book.)* No, not especially.

THE
MOTHER: Can you tell me why he didn't leave anything then . . . he had an annual income of twenty thousand in the last couple of years.

THE SON: I don't know anything about father's business, but he did say that the house was expensive and he bought all this furniture recently, of course.

THE MOTHER:	Is that what he said? I wonder if he had any debts.
THE SON:	I don't know. I know he'd had some debts earlier, but they were paid off when he died.
THE MOTHER:	Where did all the money disappear to then? Had he written a will? He hated me, of course, and he often threatened to leave me without a penny. Is it possible, do you think, that he could have hidden his savings somewhere? *(Pause)* Is someone walking about out there?
THE SON:	No, I can't hear anything.
THE MOTHER:	I've got a bit nervous from all these upsets lately . . . the funeral and the business and . . . anyway, you know your sister is going to take over this apartment so you'd better look for a furnished room somewhere.
THE SON:	Yes, I know.
THE MOTHER:	You don't like your brother-in-law?
THE SON:	No, I don't like him.
THE MOTHER:	But he's a good boy and very clever. You should like him. He deserves it.
THE SON:	He doesn't like me either . . . and besides, he wasn't very nice towards father.
THE MOTHER:	Whose fault was that?
THE SON:	Father wasn't unkind towards him.
THE MOTHER:	Wasn't he?
THE SON:	I thought I heard someone walking about outside.
THE MOTHER:	Light a couple of lamps. But only a couple, mind you! *(The Son lights a couple of electric lamps. Pause.)* Can't

you put the portrait of father in your room? The one hanging on the wall over there.

THE SON: Why should I do that?

THE
MOTHER: I don't like it; his eyes are so cold.

THE SON: I don't think so.

THE
MOTHER: Take it away. You appreciate it so you shall have it.

THE SON: *(Takes the portrait down.)* Yes, I will.

             Pause.

THE
MOTHER: I'm expecting Axel and Gerda back . . . do you want to meet them?

THE SON: No . . . I'm not looking forward to . . . I'll disappear into my room . . . but I'd like to light my stove in there.

THE
MOTHER: We can't afford to burn up our money like that . . .

THE SON: You've said that for twenty years now, but when it comes to going on ostentatious trips abroad there is never any shortage of money, and we can afford to dine in restaurants for a hundred *kronor* a time or the equivalent of four cords of birch logs; imagine four cords of birch logs for the price of one dinner.

THE
MOTHER: Nonsense!

THE SON: Yes, something went very wrong in this house, but I expect it's all over now . . . it's just the settlement left . . .

THE
MOTHER: What do you mean?

THE SON: I mean the estate inventory and all the rest . . .

THE
MOTHER: What . . . the rest?

THE SON: Debts and unfinished matters . . .

THE MOTHER:	I see.
THE SON:	Anyway, can I have some money for some warmer clothes, please?
THE MOTHER:	How can you ask for that now? Isn't it about time you earned your own money?
THE SON:	I must get my degree first.
THE MOTHER:	You'll have to borrow like everyone else.
THE SON:	Who'll want to lend me money?
THE MOTHER:	Your father's friends.
THE SON:	He didn't have any friends. An independent man cannot have any friends, because friendship implies mutual admiration . . .
THE MOTHER:	How wise you are. You must have got that from your father.
THE SON:	Yes, he was a wise man who happened to do some foolish things in his time.
THE MOTHER:	Listen to you! Do you have any plans to get married!
THE SON:	No, thank you. I'm not going to keep a lady companion for young gentlemen, or be a courtesan's legal guardian, equip my best friend – i.e. my worst enemy – for war against myself . . . No, I proceed with caution.
THE MOTHER:	What are you saying? You'd better go into your room. I've had enough of you for today. I believe you've been drinking.
THE SON:	I always need a drink, partly for my cough and partly to make up for the lack of food.
THE MOTHER:	Something wrong with the food again?

THE SON: No, there's nothing wrong, but it's so insubstantial, it tastes like air.

THE
MOTHER: *(Amazed)* You'd better go now!

THE SON: Or else . . . there are so many spices in it that they make you hungry. It's like eating spiced air.

THE
MOTHER: I do believe you're drunk. Go away.

THE SON: Yes, I shall go. I was going to say something but that will have to wait until some other time. Yes . . . *(Exits)*

> *The Mother nervously walks up and down, pulls out drawers.*

> *Son-in-law enters quickly.*

THE
MOTHER: *(Greeting him warmly.)* At last! There you are, Axel. I've missed you terribly, but where is Gerda?

SON-IN-LAW: She'll be along in a minute. How are you, how are things?

THE
MOTHER: Sit down and let me ask you first. We haven't seen each other since the wedding. – Why are you back so soon? You said you were going to be away for eight days and you're back after only three.

SON-IN-LAW: Well . . . it got a bit boring . . . you know, when we'd covered most subjects we felt a bit lonely . . . we were so used to your company . . . we missed you.

THE
MOTHER: Really? I suppose the three of us have been through thick and thin and maybe I've been of some use to you both.

SON-IN-LAW: Gerda is a child, she doesn't understand the art of living, she's prejudiced and she can be a little stubborn . . . fanatical even, in some ways . . .

THE
MOTHER: But what did you think of the wedding?

SON-IN-LAW: A great success. A great success. And the verses, how did you like them?

THE
MOTHER: The verses dedicated to me, you mean? It's not every mother-in-law who gets verses like that on her daughter's wedding . . . you know the one about the pelican who gives her blood to her young . . . I cried, yes, I did . . .

SON-IN-LAW: At first yes, but afterwards you danced every dance, Gerda was almost jealous of you . . .

THE
MOTHER: That wouldn't be the first time either . . . she wanted me to come dressed in black, because I'm in mourning, but I wasn't going to have any of that. How would it look if I started to obey my own children?

SON-IN-LAW: No, that wouldn't do at all. Gerda is a little silly at times. I can't as much as look at another woman . . .

THE
MOTHER: What? Aren't you happy together?

SON-IN-LAW: Happy? What does that word mean?

THE
MOTHER: I see. So you've been quarrelling already?

SON-IN-LAW: Already? We did nothing but quarrel throughout our engagement . . . and now this thing happened . . . about resigning my commission and becoming a lieutenant in the reserve . . . it's funny but she seemed to prefer me in uniform . . .

THE
MOTHER: Why don't you wear your uniform then? I must admit I hardly recognize you in civilian clothes. You seem to be a completely different person . . .

SON-IN-LAW: I'm only allowed to wear uniform when on duty and on parade . . .

THE
MOTHER: Allowed?

SON-IN-LAW: Yes, there are regulations . . .

THE
MOTHER: Anyway, I feel sorry for Gerda; she got engaged to a
               lieutenant and married a book-keeper.

SON-IN-LAW: What can I do about that? One has to live after all.
               Talking of living . . . how is the state of the business?

THE
MOTHER: I don't know, to tell you the truth. But I have my
               suspicions about Fredrik.

SON-IN-LAW: In what way?

THE
MOTHER: He said such strange things here this evening.

SON-IN-LAW: That blockhead . . .

THE
MOTHER: They are usually a sly lot, and I'm not sure whether
               there is a will or whether he's hidden his savings
               somewhere . . .

SON-IN-LAW: Have you had a look round?

THE
MOTHER: I've looked in all his drawers . . .

SON-IN-LAW: In the boy's?

THE
MOTHER: Yes, of course and I always look through his waste
               paper basket because he writes letters and then he tears
               them up . . .

SON-IN-LAW: There's nothing there, but have you looked through the
               old man's secretaire?

THE
MOTHER: Yes, of course . . .

SON-IN-LAW: But properly? All the drawers?

THE
MOTHER: All of them!

SON-IN-LAW: But secretaires usually have secret drawers.

THE
MOTHER: I didn't think of that.

SON-IN-LAW: Let's have a look then.

THE
MOTHER: No, don't touch it, it has to be kept sealed until after
              the inventory proceedings.

SON-IN-LAW: Can't we get round the seal?

THE
MOTHER: No, it's impossible.

SON-IN-LAW: If we loosen the boards at the back . . . secret drawers
              are always at the back . . .

THE
MOTHER: We need tools for that . . .

SON-IN-LAW: Oh no. We'll manage without . . .

THE
MOTHER: But we mustn't tell Gerda.

SON-IN-LAW: Of course not. She'd soon tell her brother . . .

THE
MOTHER: *(Closing the doors.)* I'll close the door just to be on the
              safe side . . .

SON-IN-LAW: *(Examines the secretaire at the back.)* Someone's been
              here already. The back is loose . . . I can put my hand
              through . . .

THE
MOTHER: It must be the boy . . . you see, just as I suspected . . .
              hurry up, someone's coming . . .

SON-IN-LAW: There are some papers here . . .

THE
MOTHER: Hurry up, someone's coming . . .

SON-IN-LAW: A large envelope . . .

THE
MOTHER: Gerda is coming. Give me the papers . . . quickly.

SON-IN-LAW: *(Hands over a large envelope which the mother hides.)*
              Here. Put it away.

              *At first someone tries to open the door, then there is a
              hard knock.*

SON-IN-LAW: Why did you have to lock the door . . . now we're lost.

THE
MOTHER: Be quiet.

SON-IN-LAW: You're stupid . . . unlock the door! Or I'll do it. Get
            out of the way.

                    He opens the door.

GERDA: *(Enters, downcast.)* Why did you lock the door?

THE
MOTHER: Aren't you going to say hello first, darling, I haven't
            seen you since the wedding. Did you have a nice
            honeymoon? Tell mumsy about it and don't look so
            miserable.

GERDA: *(Sits down in a chair, depressed.)* Why did you lock the
            door?

THE
MOTHER: Because it kept on banging and I got tired of telling
            people to close the door after them every time. Shall we
            discuss how to decorate your flat? You are going to live
            here, aren't you?

GERDA: I suppose we have to . . . I don't care anyway . . . what
            do you say, Axel?

SON-IN-LAW: I'm sure this will be fine and mother-in-law will be
            comfortable too . . . since we all get on so well . . .

GERDA: Where are you going to live then, mother?

THE
MOTHER: Here my darling, I'll just put a bed in here.

SON-IN-LAW: Are you going to put a bed in here, darling . . . in the
            drawing-room?

GERDA: Are you talking to me?

SON-IN-LAW: I expect it will be alright . . . we'll all have to lend a
            helping hand and mother-in-law will contribute
            towards the food and rent.

GERDA: *(Brightens up.)* And I'll get some extra help . . .

THE
MOTHER: Yes of course, my child . . . as long as I don't have to
             wash up.

GERDA: Oh no. I'm sure it's going to work out alright, as long
             as I'm allowed to keep my husband to myself. They
             mustn't look at him . . . the way they did at that
             boarding-house all the time, that's why we cut short
             the holiday, but I'll kill anyone who tries to take him
             away from me. So now you know.

THE
MOTHER: Let's start moving the furniture . . .

SON-IN-LAW: *(Stares at the Mother.)* Fine . . . Gerda can start in here
             . . .

GERDA: Why? I don't like being alone in here . . . I won't feel
             at ease until we've moved in properly . . .

SON-IN-LAW: Since you're both afraid of the dark I suggest we all
             stick together . . .

             They all exit.

SCENE TWO

*The stage is empty; the wind is blowing outside, howling through the
windows and the tiled stove; the door at the back starts to flap, papers fly
about the room, a palm on a whatnot starts to shake furiously, a
photograph falls down from the wall. The Son's voice can be heard:
"Mother" and soon afterwards: "Shut the door!" Pause. The rocking-
chair moves.*

THE
MOTHER: *(Enters, agitated with a piece of paper in her hand.)*
             What's this? The rocking-chair is moving by itself.

SON-IN-LAW: *(After her.)* What was it? What does it say? Can I read?
             Is it a will?

THE
MOTHER: Shut the door. We're blowing away. I must open a
             window to get rid of the smell. It wasn't a will . . . it
             was a letter addressed to the boy . . . he lies about me
             . . . and you.

SON-IN-LAW: Can I read it?

THE
MOTHER: No, it will only poison you, I'll tear it up, lucky it
              didn't reach him . . . *(She tears the paper and throws it
              in the tiled stove.)* Imagine, he rises from the dead and
              speaks from the grave . . . he's not dead. I can't live
              here any longer . . . He says that I've murdered him
              . . . that's not true. He died of a stroke, that's what the
              doctor said . . . but he claims other things too. Axel,
              you must see to it that we get out of this apartment, I
              can't stand it any longer. Promise me that, won't you!
              Look at the rocking-chair!

SON-IN-LAW: It's the through-draught.

THE
MOTHER: Let's get away from here. Promise.

SON-IN-LAW: I can't do that . . . I was relying on this money . . . you
              were hinting . . . otherwise I wouldn't have got married
              . . . now we must accept things as they are; I feel
              cheated and I'm a ruined man. We must stick together
              in order to survive, we must economize now and you'll
              have to help us.

THE
MOTHER: You mean I should work as a maid in my own home? I
              won't do that.

SON-IN-LAW: Beggars can't be choosers . . .

THE
MOTHER: You're a scrounger.

SON-IN-LAW: Shut up, you old bag.

THE
MOTHER: Your maid indeed!

SON-IN-LAW: That may teach you how your own maids must have
              felt, when they had to starve and shiver, unlike you . . .

THE
MOTHER: I have my annuity . . .

SON-IN-LAW: That wouldn't even pay for an attic room, but it will go
              towards the rent here if we stay put . . . and if you
              don't, I'll leave.

THE
MOTHER: You'll leave Gerda? You've never loved her . . .

SON-IN-LAW: You should know . . . you wiped her out of my mind,
you pushed her out of the way . . . except the bedroom
which she was allowed to keep to herself . . . and if we
have a child you'll take that away from her as well . . .
She doesn't know anything yet, doesn't understand
anything, but she's beginning to wake up from her
sleep-walking state. You'd better watch out when she
opens her eyes.

THE
MOTHER: Axel! We must stick together . . . we mustn't go our
separate ways . . . I can't live alone, I'll agree to
anything except the chaise-longue . . .

SON-IN-LAW: No! I don't want to ruin the whole apartment by
having a bed in here . . . and that's final.

THE
MOTHER: But let me have another chaise-longue at least.

SON-IN-LAW: No, we can't afford that, and this is a lovely piece of
furniture, anyway.

THE
MOTHER: Ugh! It is a bloody butcher's block.

SON-IN-LAW: Nonsense . . . but if you don't like it . . . your
alternatives are solitary confinement in the attic . . . the
chapel or the poor-house.

THE
MOTHER: I give in!

SON-IN-LAW: You'd better . . .

              Pause.

THE
MOTHER: I can't get over it . . . he wrote and told his son that
we'd killed him.

SON-IN-LAW: There are many ways of murdering a person . . . and
your way had the advantage of not being listed under
the criminal code.

THE
MOTHER: Why don't you say *ours*. You helped by getting him into a rage and bringing him to despair . . .

SON-IN-LAW: He was an obstacle in our way and he didn't want to step aside, so I had to push him . . .

THE
MOTHER: The only thing I reproach you with is that you tempted me away from my home . . . and I'll never forget that evening, the first evening I spent in your house . . . when we were sitting down to a festive table and we heard those ghastly screams from the plantation outside and we thought they were coming from the prison yard or the madhouse, do you remember? It was him walking about in the tobacco fields in the dark with the rain pouring down – howling for his wife and children . . .

SON-IN-LAW: Why do you bring that up now? And how do you know it was him?

THE
MOTHER: He said so in his letter.

SON-IN-LAW: It doesn't affect us. He was no angel himself . . .

THE
MOTHER: No, that's true enough, but he had human feelings after all . . . more than you sometimes . . .

SON-IN-LAW: Your sympathies begin to shift . . .

THE
MOTHER: Don't be angry with me now. We must be friends.

SON-IN-LAW: Yes, we must, we are doomed . . .

Hoarse cries from another room.

THE
MOTHER: What's that? Did you hear? It's him . . .

SON-IN-LAW: *(Harshly)* Which him? *(The Mother listens.)* Who is it? The boy! He must have been drinking again.

THE
MOTHER: Is it Fredrik? It sounded just like him, I thought for a moment . . . I can't stand this. What's the matter with him?

SON-IN-LAW: Go and have a look. I expect the savage is drunk again.

THE
MOTHER: Don't talk about him like that. He's my son, after all.

SON-IN-LAW: Yours anyway. *(Takes out his watch.)*

THE
MOTHER: Why are you looking at your watch? Don't you want to stay for supper?

SON-IN-LAW: No thank you, I don't enjoy weak tea and I never eat rancid anchovy . . . or porridge . . . besides, I'm going to a meeting . . .

THE
MOTHER: What kind of a meeting?

SON-IN-LAW: A business meeting which has nothing to do with you. Are you playing the part of mother-in-law now?

THE
MOTHER: You don't mind leaving your wife on her own the first evening?

SON-IN-LAW: That's none of your business.

THE
MOTHER: Now I know what to expect . . . for myself and my children. It's time to take off the masks . . .

SON-IN-LAW: You're right.

SCENE THREE

The same decor as before. Someone is playing the piano outside. Godard's: "Berceuse" from Jocelyn. Gerda is sitting at the desk. Long pause.

THE SON: *(Enters)* Are you alone?

GERDA: Yes, mummy's in the kitchen.

THE SON: Where is Axel then?

GERDA: He's at a meeting . . . sit down and talk to me, Fredrik, keep me company.

THE SON: *(Sits down.)* Yes, I don't think we've ever really talked
            before, we always seemed to avoid each other, there's
            been a feeling of mistrust . . .

GERDA: You always sided with father, and I with mother.

THE SON: Maybe that will change now. Do you feel you really
            knew father?

GERDA: What a strange question. I only saw him through
            mother's eyes . . .

THE SON: But you could tell that he was fond of you.

GERDA: Why did he want me to break off my engagement then?

THE SON: Because he didn't think your husband would give you
            the support you needed.

GERDA: He got punished for that when mummy left him.

THE SON: Was it your husband who was behind her leaving?

GERDA: Both of us. We wanted to teach daddy a lesson when
            he tried to separate me from my husband.

THE SON: That shortened his life, though . . . and believe me, he
            only wanted what was best for you.

GERDA: You stayed with him. What did he say, how did he
            react?

THE SON: I can't tell you the agony he went through . . .

GERDA: But what did he say about mummy?

THE SON: Nothing . . . I'll tell you something though . . . after all
            I've seen I'm definitely not going to get married, that's
            for sure. *(Pause)* Are you happy, Gerda?

GERDA: Yes. When you've got the man you wanted, you're
            happy.

THE SON: Why is your husband leaving you alone on your first
            evening back then?

GERDA: He's got some business to attend to, a meeting.

THE SON: At a restaurant?

GERDA: What did you say? Are you sure?

THE SON: I thought you knew.

GERDA: *(Cries, hiding her face in her hands.)* Oh, my God, my
             God!

THE SON: I'm sorry if I hurt you.

GERDA: Yes, you hurt me, you hurt me terribly! Oh, I want to
             die!

THE SON: Why didn't you stay away longer?

GERDA: He was worried about business, he missed mummy, he
             can't be away from her . . .

             They stare at each other.

THE SON: I see. *(Pause)* Was it a pleasant trip apart from that?

GERDA: Yes.

THE SON: Poor Gerda!

GERDA: What are you saying?

THE SON: As you know, mother is curious, and she knows how to
             use the telephone.

GERDA: What? Has she been spying?

THE SON: She's always spying . . . she's probably listening to us
             behind the door this very moment . . .

GERDA: You always think badly of mother.

THE SON: And you always think well of her. How is that? You
             know her character, after all . . .

GERDA: No, I don't. And I don't want to know . . .

THE SON: There was something else, you didn't want . . . there's
             a reason for it . . .

GERDA: Be quiet. I know I'm sleep-walking, but I don't want
             to be woken up. Because then I wouldn't be able to go
             on living.

THE SON: Don't you think we're all sleep-walkers? In my law
             studies I read about serious criminals who can't explain
             how it happened . . . they didn't think they were doing
             anything wrong until they were caught in the act and
             then they woke up. If it's not a dream, it's certainly
             some kind of sleep.

GERDA: Let me sleep. I know I'll have to wake up one day, but
           I hope it won't be for a long time. Oh, I have this
           awful feeling . . . but no proof . . . Do you remember
           when we were children . . . people called us wicked if
           we told the truth . . . you're so wicked, they always
           told me when I called something bad that really *was*
           bad . . . so I learnt to keep quiet . . . and I was praised
           for my good behaviour after that. That's how I learnt
           to dissemble and after that I was ready to step into the
           world.

THE SON: One must cover up one's neighbour's faults and
           weaknesses, certainly . . . but the next step is flight and
           flattery . . . sometimes it's one's duty to speak up . . .

GERDA: Be quiet.

THE SON: I *am* going to be quiet.

           Pause.

GERDA: No. I'd rather you talked, but not about that! I can
           hear your thoughts in the silence. When people get
           together they speak, they speak all the time to conceal
           their thoughts . . . to forget, to make themselves deaf
           . . . they want to hear the news about other people but
           they prefer to keep quiet about themselves.

THE SON: Poor Gerda!

GERDA: Do you know what hurts most? *(Pause)* Seeing the
           futility of the greatest happiness.

THE SON: There was a true word.

GERDA: I'm cold. Please light a fire.

THE SON: Are you cold as well?

GERDA: I'm always cold and hungry.

THE SON: You too. It's a strange house. But if I go out and fetch
           some logs now we'll be told off for a week at least.

GERDA: Maybe someone has prepared the fire. Mother
           sometimes used to put some logs in just to tease us . . .

           *The Son walks over to the tiled stove and opens the
           doors.*

THE SON: There are a couple of logs here, actually . . . *(Pause)*
            But what's this? A letter . . . torn. We could use that to
            light the fire . . .

GERDA: Fredrik, don't light it, she'll tell us off. Come and sit
            down again, let's talk . . . *(The Son sits down beside her,
            puts the letter on the table in front of him. Pause.)* Do
            you know why father hated my husband the way he
            did?

THE SON: Yes, because your Axel took his daughter and wife
            away from him and left him on his own, and then he
            noticed how the son-in-law got better fed than he, and
            you locked yourselves in the drawing-room, played
            your music and read your books . . . things that father
            wasn't interested in; he was pushed out of the way,
            robbed of food in his own house . . . that's why he
            went to restaurants and clubs in the end.

GERDA: We didn't think . . . poor daddy. – It's nice to have
            parents of such impeccable reputation and we must be
            grateful . . . do you remember their silver wedding . . .
            the speeches and verses that people addressed to them?

THE SON: I remember, but I thought it was a bit of a farce
            celebrating 'the happy marriage' when in fact they had
            fought like cat and dog . . .

GERDA: Fredrik!

THE SON: I can't help it, you know how they lived . . . don't you
            remember when mother wanted to jump through the
            window and we had to hold her back . . .

GERDA: Be quiet.

THE SON: There were reasons that we don't know about . . . and
            during the divorce when I was looking after the old
            man he seemed to want to open his heart several times,
            but the words never came across his lips . . . I dream
            about him sometimes . . .

GERDA: So do I. I see him as a thirty year-old and he gives me
            a friendly look, full of meaning, but I don't understand
            what he wants . . . sometimes mummy is with him; he's
            not angry with her because he was very fond of her
            right up to the end. You remember how beautifully he

spoke of her at the silver wedding, how he thanked her despite everything . . .

THE SON: Despite everything . . . That says a lot and yet not enough.

GERDA: But it was a beautiful speech. She did have one great merit . . . she was a good housekeeper.

THE SON: I think that's debatable.

GERDA: What do you mean?

THE SON: Now you're on her side. As soon as there's talk about housekeeping you're always on the same side . . . it's like freemasonry or Camorra . . . I've even asked old Margret – who is my friend – about the housekeeping money, and I've asked her why we never get enough food here . . . but she just clams up, the garrulous old fool, she clams up and gets angry . . . can you tell me why?

GERDA: No.

THE SON: So you're a freemason too.

GERDA: I don't understand what you mean.

THE SON: Sometimes I wonder if father is a victim of this Secret Society which he must have discovered.

GERDA: You speak like a madman sometimes.

THE SON: I remember that father used the word Camorra occasionally, as a joke, but in the end he didn't say anything . . .

GERDA: How terribly cold it is in here, deathly cold . . .

THE SON: I'll light the fire then. Never mind the consequences. *(He picks up the torn letter distractedly at first and then he starts to read it.)* What's this? *(Pause)* To my son . . . In my father's handwriting. Addressed to me? *(He reads. Collapses onto a chair and continues in silence.)*

GERDA: What are you reading? What is it?

THE SON: It's terrible. *(Pause)* It's quite dreadful.

GERDA: Tell me what it is.

Pause.

THE SON:	It's too much . . . *(To Gerda.)* It's a letter from our dead father, to me. *(Reads on.)* Now I'm waking up from my sleep.

> *He throws himself on the chaise-longue and howls in pain, but puts the letter in his pocket.*

GERDA:	*(Kneeling beside him.)* What is it, Fredrik? Tell me what it is. Little brother, are you ill, tell me, tell me.
THE SON:	*(Gets up.)* I can't go on living any more.
GERDA:	Tell me what it is.
THE SON:	It's incredible . . . *(Collects himself, gets up.)*
GERDA:	Maybe it's not true.
THE SON:	*(Irritated)* He wouldn't lie from the grave . . .
GERDA:	Maybe he was plagued by a sick imagination . . .
THE SON:	Your secret conspiracy again. Then I'll tell you. Listen now . . .
GERDA:	I think I know it all already, but I don't believe it.
THE SON:	You don't want to. But this is how it is. She who gave us life is a thief.
GERDA:	No.
THE SON:	She stole from the housekeeping money, she made up bills, she bought the worst food for the highest price, she had her main meal in the kitchen in the morning and gave us food that was diluted and heated up . . . she creamed off the milk . . . that's why we're so weak, always sick and hungry, the money allocated for heating was used for other things . . . that's why we were cold. When father discovered all this he warned her and she promised to improve but she carried on in the same way and thought up new things – the soya sauce and the cayenne pepper.
GERDA:	I don't believe a word of it.
THE SON:	Conspiracy. But here comes the worst. The shabby fellow who is now your husband, Gerda, he has never loved you, he loved your mother.
GERDA:	No!

THE SON: When father discovered that and when your husband borrowed money from mother, our mother, that monster covered up by proposing to you. This is the gist of the story . . . you can fill in the details yourself.

GERDA: *(Cries in her handkerchief.)* I realised all this before but it didn't sink in, because it was too much.

THE SON: What can we do now to save you from further humiliation?

GERDA: I must go away.

THE SON: Where to?

GERDA: I don't know. ·

THE SON: Wait and see how the whole thing unfolds.

GERDA: But you can't attack your own mother, she is sacred . . .

THE SON: The devil she is!

GERDA: Don't say that.

THE SON: She is a cunning beast, but her egotism often blinds her . . .

GERDA: Let's run away.

THE SON: Where to? No, Let's stay until that terrible cheat drives her away. Shhh, he's coming. Shhh! Gerda, let's practice our own bit of freemasonry now. I'll tell you when. And remember: He beat you on the wedding night.

GERDA: Remind me of that often, or I'll forget. I would so like to forget.

THE SON: Our lives are ruined, nothing to respect, look up to . . . we can't forget . . . let us make amends and honour the memory of our father.

GERDA: And see that justice is being done.

THE SON: You mean revenge.

The Son-in-law enters.

GERDA: *(Dissembles)* Good evening. Was it a good meeting? Did you have a nice meal?

SON-IN-LAW: It was cancelled.

GERDA: Was it closed, did you say?

SON-IN-LAW: Cancelled, I said.

GERDA: Are you going to look after the house now then?

SON-IN-LAW: You're funny tonight, I suppose Fredrik is entertaining
                      company.

GERDA: We've played at freemasonry.

SON-IN-LAW: That's nothing to joke about.

THE SON: Let's play Camorra instead then. Or vendetta.

SON-IN-LAW: *(Ill-at-ease)* What strange talk, what are you two up to;
                      do you have secrets between you?

GERDA: You wouldn't let us in on your secrets, would you? Or
                      maybe you don't have any secrets?

SON-IN-LAW: What's happened? Has someone been here?

THE SON: Gerda and I have been visited by a dead spirit.

SON-IN-LAW: The joke's wearing a little thin. It doesn't bode well to
                      joke about that sort of thing. But it suits you to be a
                      little cheerful for a change, Gerda; you're so glum most
                      of the time . . . *(He wants to pat her cheek but she
                      withdraws.)* Are you afraid of me?

GERDA: Not at all. There are feelings which may look like fear
                      but are something quite different . . . there are gestures
                      which say more than facial expressions and there are
                      words which conceal what neither gestures nor
                      expressions can disclose . . .

                      Son-in-law, surprised, touches a bookshelf.

                      *The Son gets up from the rocking-chair which carries on
                      rocking until the Mother enters.*

THE SON: Here comes mother with the porridge.

SON-IN-LAW: Is it . . .

THE
MOTHER: *(Enters, catches sight of the rocking-chair, is frightened at
                      first but calms down later.)* Do you want to come and
                      have your porridge?

SON-IN-LAW: No thank you. If it's oats give it to the dogs, if you have any; if it's rye put it on your boils . . .

THE
MOTHER: We're poor and we must economize . . .

SON-IN-LAW: You're not poor if you earn twenty thousand a year . . .

THE SON: You are if you lend money to people who won't pay you back.

SON-IN-LAW: What's this? Has the boy gone mad?

THE SON: Maybe he was mad before.

THE
MOTHER: Are you coming now?

GERDA: Come, let's go. Courage, gentlemen . . . I'm going to give you a sandwich and a piece of steak . . .

THE
MOTHER: You?

GERDA: Yes, me. In my own home . . .

THE
MOTHER: There's a thing.

GERDA: *(Pointing to the door.)* After you, gentlemen . . .

SON-IN-LAW: *(To the Mother.)* What's this supposed to mean?

THE
MOTHER: I smell a rat.

SON-IN-LAW: You're not far wrong.

GERDA: After you, gentlemen!

Everybody goes towards the door.

THE
MOTHER: *(To the Son-in-law.)* Did you see how the rocking-chair moved? His rocking-chair?

SON-IN-LAW: No, I didn't. But I saw something else.

SCENE FOUR

The same decor as before. The waltz "Il Me Disait" by Ferraris is being played.

Gerda is sitting down with a book.

THE MOTHER:	*(Enters)* Do you recognize it?
GERDA:	The waltz? Yes.
THE MOTHER:	Your wedding waltz which I danced to the whole night long.
GERDA:	You danced? – Where is Axel?
THE MOTHER:	How should I know?
GERDA:	There, there. Have you been quarrelling already?
	Pause. They look at each other without saying anything.
THE MOTHER:	What are you reading, darling?
GERDA:	The cook book. But why don't they tell you how long things should cook for?
THE MOTHER:	*(Modestly)* It varies so much, you see. People have different tastes, one person wants it this way and another person that way . . .
GERDA:	I don't see that at all; food should be served freshly cooked, or it will have to be heated up, consequently spoilt. Yesterday, for instance, you cooked some grouse for three hours; for the first hour there was a lovely smell of game in the whole apartment and then silence descended on the kitchen; and when the food was served it lacked all aroma and tasted of air. Can you explain why?
THE MOTHER:	*(Bashful)* I don't understand.

GERDA: Explain why there was no sauce then, where did it
            disappear to, who finished it?

THE
MOTHER: I don't understand anything.

GERDA: But I've been asking around, you see, and now I know
            a lot of things . . .

THE
MOTHER: (Interrupts) I know but you can't teach me anything
            . . . I'll teach you about the art of housekeeping . . .

GERDA: Do you mean about soya sauce and cayenne pepper? I
            know about that already . . . and choosing dishes for
            dinner parties that no one will want so that you'll have
            food left over for the following day . . . or inviting
            people when the larder is only full of left-overs . . . I
            know all that now and that's why I'll take over the
            cooking from today.

THE
MOTHER: (Furious) Do you mean I shall be your maid?

GERDA: I'll be yours and you'll be mine. We'll do it together.
            Here's Axel.

SON-IN-LAW: (Enters with a sturdy stick in his hand.) Well? What do
            you think of the chaise-longue?

THE
MOTHER: I don't know what to say . . .

SON-IN-LAW: (Menacing) Isn't it good enough? Is something amiss?

THE
MOTHER: Now I begin to understand.

SON-IN-LAW: Do you? As we don't seem to get enough food in this
            house, Gerda and I intend to eat by ourselves from
            now on.

THE
MOTHER: What about me?

SON-IN-LAW: You're as fat as a pig so you don't need very much.
            You ought to think of your health and slim down a
            little, like we had to do. Just leave us alone for a
            moment, Gerda . . . (Addressing the Mother.) I'm going
            to ask you to light a fire!

Gerda leaves.

THE
MOTHER: *(Trembling with rage.)* I believe there are some logs over
              there . . .

SON-IN-LAW: Oh no . . . a few sticks perhaps but I want you to go
            and fetch some real logs and fill the whole stove with
            them.

THE
MOTHER: *(Hesitates)* Are we going to burn up our money?

SON-IN-LAW: No, but we must burn logs in order to get warm.
            Hurry up. *(The Mother doesn't move.)* One, two, three.
            (Beats his stick on the table.)

THE
MOTHER: I don't think there are any logs left.

SON-IN-LAW: You're either lying or you've stolen the money for the
            firewood . . . we bought a whole cord the day before
            yesterday.

THE
MOTHER: Now I see your true nature . . .

SON-IN-LAW: *(Sits down in the rocking-chair.)* You would have noticed
            that a long time ago, if your age and experience had not
            duped me . . . quickly, go and fetch some logs or else
            . . . *(Lifts the stick.)*

          *The Mother leaves, comes back immediately with some
          logs.*

SON-IN-LAW: Light a proper fire now and don't cheat. One, two,
            three.

THE
MOTHER: How like the old man you are now . . . sitting there in
              his rocking-chair like that.

SON-IN-LAW: Light it!

THE
MOTHER: *(With suppressed anger.)* I shall, I shall.

SON-IN-LAW: And now you keep an eye on the fire while we go into
            the dining-room and have something to eat . . .

THE
MOTHER: What am I going to have to eat then?

SON-IN-LAW: The porridge that Gerda has put out for you in the
kitchen.

THE
MOTHER: With blue skimmed milk . . .

SON-IN-LAW: After you've creamed off the best, yes, that's only right
and proper.

THE
MOTHER: *(Darkly)* I'll leave.

SON-IN-LAW: You can't, because I'll lock you up in here.

THE
MOTHER: *(Whispers)* Then I'll jump out of the window.

SON-IN-LAW: Do . . . by all means. You should have done that ages
ago, then four people's lives could have been saved.
Light the fire now. Blow on it. Like that, yes. Sit down
here now until we get back. *(Leaves)*

    Pause.

    *The Mother stops the rocking-chair first, then listens
at the door, takes some of the logs out of the fire again
and hides them under the chaise-longue.*

    The Son enters a little drunk.

THE
MOTHER: *(Reacts)* Is that you?

THE SON: *(Sits down in the rocking-chair.)* Yes.

THE
MOTHER: How are you?

THE SON: Terrible, it's all over with me soon.

THE
MOTHER: It's just your imagination. Don't rock like that. Look at
me, I've reached a . . . a certain age . . . and I've
worked and toiled for my children and my home all my
life, haven't I?

THE SON: Oh! And the pelican never gave from her heart's blood.
My zoology book says it's all a lie.

THE
MOTHER: What's your complaint then?

THE SON: Listen mother, if I was sober I wouldn't answer
               truthfully because I wouldn't have the strength but
               now I'm going to tell you that I've read father's letter
               which you stole and threw on the fire . . .

THE
MOTHER: What are you saying, what letter?

THE SON: Always lying. I remember when you taught me to lie
               for the first time. I could hardly speak, do you
               remember?

THE
MOTHER: No, I don't remember. Don't rock like that!

THE SON: And when you lied to me for the first time. I also
               remember once when I was a child . . . I had hidden
               under the piano and then a lady came to see you. You
               sat there, lying to her for three hours and I had to
               listen to you.

THE
MOTHER: It's not true.

THE SON: But do you know why I am so wretched? I was never
               breast-fed, you gave me a nanny and a bottle instead;
               and when I got older nanny took me to her sister's and
               she was a prostitute; and there I witnessed the most
               intimate scenes, the kind that usually only dog owners
               show children in the streets in spring and autumn.
               When I told you about it . . . I was four at the time
               . . . when I told you what I had seen in that den of
               vice you said I was lying and you hit me as if I'd been
               lying even though I spoke the truth. This maid –
               encouraged by you – initiated me into all the secrets
               when I was five years old . . . I was only five . . . *(He
               sobs.)* And then I starved and froze, like father and the
               rest of the family. And it's only now . . . all these years
               later . . . I learn that you stole from the housekeeping
               money and the money for the heating . . . look at me,
               pelican, look at Gerda who hasn't got a chest. You
               know perfectly well how you murdered my father, you
               know . . . because you brought him to despair which is

not a crime punishable by law; you know yourself how
you've murdered my sister, but now she realises it as
well.

THE
MOTHER: Don't rock! What does she know?

THE SON: The same as you, but I can't say it. *(Sobs)* It's terrible
to have to say all this, but I had to. I know that when
I'm sober again I'll shoot myself, that's why I carry on
drinking. I don't dare get sober . . .

THE
MOTHER: Go on lying.

THE SON: Father once said in anger that you were one of nature's
great frauds . . . that you didn't learn to speak like
other children, but you learnt to lie . . . you always
evaded your duties because you wanted to enjoy
yourself. And I remember when Gerda was very ill . . .
we thought she was dying . . . you went to some light
entertainment that evening – I remember your words:
"Life is hard enough without having to make it harder
still." And that summer you were in Paris for three
months with father . . . going to parties so we got into
debts. Then Gerda and I stayed here in town, locked
up with two maids in this apartment. A fireman moved
into the master bedroom with the housemaid and the
marital bed was used by the charming couple . . .

THE
MOTHER: Why haven't you told me this before?

THE SON: You've forgotten that I told you and that I was
punished for telling tales . . . or lies as you called them
because as soon as you heard a true word you called it
a lie.

THE
MOTHER: *(Walks around the room like a caged wild animal.)* I have
never heard of any son who spoke to his mother like
this.

THE SON: It's a little unusual perhaps, and unnatural, I know, but
I had to tell you once and for all. You were like a
sleepwalker who couldn't be woken up, that's why you
couldn't change either. Father said that even if you

were put on the rack, you still wouldn't admit to any
misdemeanour or confess any lies that you'd told.

THE
MOTHER: Father! Do you think he was without flaws?

THE SON: He had serious faults, but not in his relationships with
his wife and children. There are other secrets about
your marriage which I've only had a vague inkling of,
I've suspected things but I've never wanted to admit to
myself even . . . father took most of those secrets with
him when he died.

THE
MOTHER: Have you finished?

THE SON: Yes, now I'm going out to have a drink . . . I'll never
pass my exam, I don't believe in the judiciary system,
laws seem to be written by thieves and murderers in
order to set the criminals free; one true witness is not
sufficient, but two false witnesses are enough to prove a
case of guilt. At half past eleven I may be winning my
case but after twelve I've lost it; a writing error, a
missing margin can throw me into jail, even if I'm
innocent. If I show mercy towards a crook he'll punish
me by suing me for libel. My contempt for life, for
humanity, for society and myself is so immense that I
haven't got the strength to go on living . . . *(Walks
towards the door.)*

THE
MOTHER: Don't go!

THE SON: Are you afraid of the dark?

THE
MOTHER: I'm nervous.

THE SON: That follows.

THE
MOTHER: And that chair is driving me mad. It always reminded
me of two chopping knives when he sat in it . . .
chopping my heart to pieces.

THE SON: You don't have a heart.

THE
MOTHER: Don't go. I can't stay here, Axel is dishonest.

THE SON:	That's what I thought as well, until recently. But now I believe he's the victim of your criminal nature . . . yes, it was you who seduced him.
THE MOTHER:	You must be mixing in some very bad company.
THE SON:	Bad company, yes, I've never been in good company.
THE MOTHER:	Don't go.
THE SON:	What can I do here? I would only torment you to death with my talk . . .
THE MOTHER:	Don't go.
THE SON:	Are you waking up?
THE MOTHER:	Yes, now I'm waking up from a long, long sleep. It's horrible. Why didn't people wake me before?
THE SON:	That which no one could do was . . . impossible, I suppose. And as it was impossible, you couldn't help it.
THE MOTHER:	Say that again.
THE SON:	It couldn't have been any other way.
THE MOTHER:	*(Kisses his hand slavishly.)* Tell me more!
THE SON:	I don't know any more. Yes, I'm going to ask you one thing: Don't stay here and make bad things worse.
THE MOTHER:	You're right. I shall leave.
THE SON:	Poor mother.
THE MOTHER:	Do you feel sorry for me?
THE SON:	*(Sobs)* Yes, of course I do. I often used to say about you: She is so evil that I feel sorry for her.
THE MOTHER:	Thank you. Go now, Fredrik.

THE SON: Is there nothing we can do?

THE
MOTHER: No, it's irreparable.

THE SON: You're right. It's irreparable. *(Leaves)*

            Pause.

THE
MOTHER: *(Alone, with her arms across her chest for a long time.
            Then she walks to the window, opens it and looks down.
            She withdraws into the room and takes a leap to jump out
            of the window, but changes her mind when there are three
            hard knocks on the door.)* Who's that? What was that?
            (She shuts the window.) Come in! *(The doors open at the
            back.)* Is someone there? *(The Son is heard screaming
            off-stage.)* It's him in the tobacco fields. Isn't he dead?
            What shall I do, where shall I go? *(She hides behind the
            secretaire. It starts to blow again like before, papers fly
            around the room.)* Shut the window, Fredrik! *(A plant
            pot falls down.)* Shut the window. I'm freezing to death
            and the fire's gone out in the stove. *(She switches on all
            the electric lights, closes the door which opens by itself
            again, the rocking-chair moves in the wind; she walks
            round in circles and in the end she throws herself onto the
            chaise-longue and hides her face in the cushions. "Il Me
            Disait" is played outside. Gerda enters, with the porridge
            on a tray which she puts down, then she switches off all
            the electric lights except one. The Mother, waking up,
            rises.)* Don't switch the lights off.

GERDA: Yes, we must think of the expense.

THE
MOTHER: Are you back so soon?

GERDA: Yes, he didn't enjoy himself without you.

THE
MOTHER: I say!

GERDA: Here's your supper.

THE
MOTHER: I'm not hungry.

GERDA: Yes, you're hungry, but you don't like porridge.

THE
MOTHER: Yes, sometimes.

GERDA: No, never. But it's not because of that but because of
           your nasty smile every time you tormented us with that
           bowl of porridge; you enjoyed seeing us suffer . . . and
           you made the same gruel for the dog.

THE
MOTHER: I can't have that blue milk, it gives me a chill.

GERDA: That's what's left when you've creamed off the milk for
           your coffee. Here you are. *(Serves the porridge on a
           small table.)* Eat now, so I can watch you.

THE
MOTHER: I can't.

GERDA: *(Leans down and picks up some logs from behind the
           chaise-longue.)* If you don't eat up I'll show Axel that
           you've stolen these logs.

THE
MOTHER: Axel who missed my company . . . he won't harm me.
           Do you remember at the wedding when he danced with
           me . . . to "Il me disait". That's the one. *(She hums the
           second reprise which is now being played.)*

GERDA: It would be more prudent not to remind me of that
           shameful incident . . .

THE
MOTHER: And he dedicated some verses to me and gave me the
           most beautiful flowers.

GERDA: Shut up!

THE
MOTHER: Shall I recite the verses to you? I know them by heart
           . . . "In Ginnistan . . ." Ginnistan is a Persian word for
           the Garden of Eden, where gentle 'peris' live on
           exquisite scents . . . 'peris' is the same as genii or
           fairies . . . and they are made in such a way that the
           longer they live the younger they become . . .

GERDA: Oh, my God, do you think you're a 'peri'?

THE MOTHER:	Yes, it says here . . . and uncle Victor has proposed to me. What would you say if I got married again?
GERDA:	Poor mummy! You're still walking in your sleep like we've all been doing. Are you never going to wake up? Can't you see that people are laughing at you? Don't you understand when Axel insults you?
THE MOTHER:	Does he? I always think he's more polite towards me than towards you . . .
GERDA:	Even when he raised the stick at you?
THE MOTHER:	At me? It was at you, my dear.
GERDA:	Dear mother, have you lost your senses?
THE MOTHER:	He missed my company this evening, we've always had so much to talk about, he's the only person who understands me, and you're only a child . . .
GERDA:	*(Seizes her Mother by her shoulders and shakes her.)* Wake up, for God's sake.
THE MOTHER:	You're not fully grown yet, but I'm your mother and I've nourished you with my blood . . .
GERDA:	No, you gave me a bottle and stuck a dummy in my mouth. Then I had to go to the pantry and steal, but there was only rye bread which I had with mustard and when it burnt my throat I quenched my thirst with a bottle of spirit vinegar. The cruet stand and the bread basket, that was my larder.
THE MOTHER:	I see, you stole even as a child. That's nice to hear and you're not ashamed of telling me that? And I have sacrificed myself for children like these!
GERDA:	*(Cries)* I could forgive you everything, except that you took my life from me – yes, he was my life, because with him I started to live . . .

THE
MOTHER: I can't help that he preferred me. Maybe he found me
            . . . how shall I say . . . more pleasing . . . yes, he had
            better taste than your father who didn't know how to
            appreciate me until he got rivals . . . *(There are three
            hard knocks on the door.)* Who is that knocking?

GERDA: Don't say anything bad about father. I shall never be
            able to make up for what I've done to him, however
            long I live. But you're going to pay for it, because it
            was you who turned me against him. Do you remember
            when I was a little girl and you taught me to say awful
            hurtful things which I didn't understand. He was
            probably wise enough not to punish me for those
            arrows because he knew who'd shot them. Do you
            remember when you taught me to lie to him and say
            that I needed new books for school, and when you and
            I had cheated him out of money, we divided it up
            between us. How can I forget the past? Isn't there a
            draught that kills the memory without killing life? I
            wish I had the strength to leave everything behind, but
            like Fredrik . . . I'm powerless and weak . . . we're
            your victims . . . but you hardened creature can't even
            suffer for your own crimes.

THE
MOTHER: Do you know anything about my childhood? Do you
            have any idea of what a bad home I had, all the
            horrible things I learnt there. It seems it's handed
            down from one generation to the next. But who started
            it? Our first ancestors, as it said in our school-books
            and maybe that's true . . . don't blame me and I won't
            blame my parents who could blame theirs and so on.
            Anyway, it's the same story in all families, but they
            don't show it to the outside world . . .

GERDA: If that's true, I don't want to go on living but if I have
            to I'll walk through this wretched life deaf and dumb,
            in the hope that there'll be a better life after this . . .

THE
MOTHER: My dear, you do exaggerate so, but when you get a
            child of your own, you'll have other things to think
            about . . .

GERDA: I won't have any children . . .

THE MOTHER:	How do you know?
GERDA:	The doctor has told me.
THE MOTHER:	He is mistaken . . .
GERDA:	You're lying again . . . I am barren, defective, like Fredrik. That's why I don't want to go on living . . .
THE MOTHER:	You talk nonsense . . .
GERDA:	If I could follow my instinct you wouldn't be here any more. Why is it so difficult to do evil? When I raise my hand against you it's I who get hit.

The music stops abruptly. The Son is heard screaming outside.

THE MOTHER:	He's drunk again.
GERDA:	Poor Fredrik, yes . . . what's he going to do?
THE SON:	*(Enters, half drunk, stuttering.)* There appears to be . . . some smoke . . . in the kitchen!
THE MOTHER:	What did you say?
THE SON:	I think . . . I . . . I think . . . there's a fire in there.
THE MOTHER:	A fire? What are you saying?
THE SON:	Yes, I . . . think . . . there's a fire.

The Mother runs towards the back and opens the doors, but is met by a red light.

THE MOTHER:	Fire! How are we going to get out? I don't want to burn. I don't want to! *(Walks round in a circle.)*
GERDA:	*(Embraces her brother.)* Fredrik! Run, we're caught in a fire, run.
THE SON:	I can't.
GERDA:	Run! You must.

THE SON: Where to? No, I don't want to . . .

THE
MOTHER: I'd rather jump out of the window . . . *(Opens the balcony door and jumps out.)*

GERDA: Oh, my God, help us.

THE SON: That's our only hope.

GERDA: It's you who are responsible for this!

THE SON: Yes, but what else could I do? There was nothing else to do. Or was there?

GERDA: No! Everything must burn, or we won't get out of here. Hold me tight, Fredrik, hold me tight, little brother. I'm happier than I've ever been. It's getting light . . . poor mummy who was so evil, so evil . . .

THE SON: Little sister . . . poor mummy, can you feel the heat, it's lovely, I'm not cold any more, can you hear the crackling sound out there, now everything is burning, all the old things, all the nasty, old, ugly things . . .

GERDA: Hold me tight, little brother, we're not going to burn, we'll suffocate from the smoke, isn't it a nice smell, it's the palms that burn and daddy's laurel wreath, now the linen cupboard, it smells of lavender and now the roses! Little brother, don't be afraid, it's soon over, dear, dear, don't fall, poor mummy . . . who was so wicked. Hold me, tighter, hug me, like daddy used to say. It's like Christmas Eve when we used to eat in the kitchen, and dip in the pot, the only day of the year we got enough to eat, as daddy used to say . . . can you smell . . . all those lovely smells . . . it is the pantry that's burning now with the tea and the coffee and all the spices . . . the cinnamon and the cloves . . .

THE SON: *(Ecstatically)* Is it summer? The clover is in bloom, it's the beginning of the summer holidays, do you remember when we went down to the white steamers and touched them just as they'd been freshly painted. Daddy was happy then, he was alive then as he put it, and there were no more essays or compositions. That's how life should be all the time, he used to say, I think it was he who was the pelican, he plucked his feathers for us and his trousers always had worn patches at the knees and he had a worn velvet collar but we were dressed like little aristocrats . . . Gerda, hurry up, the bell's ringing on the steamer, mother is sitting in the saloon, no she's not there, poor mummy, she's gone, is she still on the quayside, where is she? I can't see her. It's no fun without mummy . . . there she is! Now the summer holidays begin.

Pause.

The doors open at the back, the strong red light becomes visible.

The Son and Gerda collapse onto the floor.

THE END

Opus 5
THE BLACK GLOVE
A lyrical fantasy for the stage in
five scenes

CHARACTERS

THE WIFE

THE TAXIDERMIST, CALLED "THE OLD MAN"

ELLEN

KRISTIN

THE CONCIERGE

THE CHRISTMAS SPIRIT

THE CHRISTMAS FAIRY

AN OLD LADY

SCENE ONE

The entrance hall.

At the back a front door with a letter box and a name plate; to the right an ice cupboard; to the left a bench.

Above the door there is a stained glass window in the shape of a heart.

A black glove lies on the floor of the vestibule.

An old gentleman enters from left, panting and puffing and sits down on the bench.

He notices the glove, picks it up with his walking stick.

OLD MAN: What's this? A glove? Black . . . a ladies' glove . . . size 6; it must belong to the young wife in there. I can tell from the marks made by the rings on the left hand . . . two plain ones and one with a rose diamond; a pretty hand . . . but with a hard grip, a silky paw with sharp claws; I'll leave it here on the ice box where the owner is bound to find it. *(The Concierge enters from left.)* Good morning to you. And Merry Christmas!

CONCIERGE: And Merry Christmas to you too, sir. I can't see very well . . . are you the gentleman with the stuffed animals?

OLD MAN: The very man, yes. I preserve birds, fishes and insects but I'm unable to preserve myself – even if I were to put arsenic soap under my skin it would crease up and I'm shedding my hair like an old sealskin trunk. My teeth are going their own way too . . .

CONCIERGE: Yes, it's like the electrical apparatus in this house; it has to be renewed and repaired all the time . . .

OLD MAN: It's unfortunate that we have to sit in the dark at Christmas time. Can't you get the lights to work?

CONCIERGE: There's been a short circuit but I may be able to put it right again soon. Let's see . . . *(Turns a switch on; the heart and the stained glass window are being lit up.)* There, now they've got light in the vestibule, anyway.

OLD MAN: You spread light around the house . . .

CONCIERGE: . . . but live in the dark basement myself. We've only got a paraffin lamp.

OLD MAN: It's good to live for other people. – What a beautiful heart!

CONCIERGE: Yes, but the colour is a little harsh . . . or shall I say . . . sharp.

OLD MAN: Sounds like a description of the young wife herself. If only she were as good as she is beautiful.

CONCIERGE: Who does that glove belong to?

OLD MAN: I found it here in the vestibule. Could you take care of it, do you think?

CONCIERGE: I'll hang it up on the board down there. I'm sure the right owner will claim it sooner or later. Now I'll move on upstairs.

OLD MAN: And I'll stay down here a little longer and rest my octogenarian body. Happy Christmas!

CONCIERGE: *(Switches the heart out and exits right.)* And to you.

          Ellen enters from right, opens the ice cupboard, takes out a rack with milk bottles.

OLD MAN: Good morning, Ellen and Happy Christmas.

ELLEN: Happy Christmas, sir.

OLD MAN: And how is the little girl and the little wife?

ELLEN: Oh, they twitter and chirp like canaries – one can hear them all the way down here even. But between you and me, the mistress isn't very nice to us. None of us is getting any Christmas bonus, not even the concierge. She says we're beasts.

OLD MAN: You shouldn't tell me things like that. I'm not part of the household. They may accuse me of gossiping.

ELLEN: Talking of canaries, have you stuffed the mistress' canary yet?

OLD MAN: Yes, I have. But . . . *(Chews)* she doesn't want to pay for it. There, now I'm telling tales, after all.

ELLEN: No, she doesn't want to pay for other people's work
            and when the master wanted to give the servants extra
            money for helping with the move back from the
            country she was beside herself. And when he gave us
            some anyway, she left the electric lights on all night
            and she left the water running. And when she didn't
            get what she wanted she pretended to be ill . . . we
            almost thought she was dying. The master had to send
            for the professor and when he came and said there was
            nothing wrong with her . . . that she was just putting it
            on . . . she wanted to take poison and threatened to
            turn the gas taps on and blow up the whole house.

OLD MAN: Oh, good Lord! What a business.

ELLEN: But in between she is like an angel. Yes, you should see
            her when she is playing with her daughter or when she
            sits there sewing her Christmas presents, like she is just
            now. I think she's possessed by the devil now and
            again. She can't help it, poor thing.

OLD MAN: You speak kindly of her, Ellen . . . I think she's ill. I've
            seen similar behaviour before. They are too well-off,
            that's the whole trouble. The husband doesn't do
            anything for a living . . . he's got a private income.

ELLEN: But he's busy all day spending his money. And this
            year he has bought three new sets of furniture for the
            drawing-room; one in black pear-wood with silver
            inlay, but now it's all been put away in the attic. Like
            you said – they're too well-off.

KRISTIN: *(Enters from right, speaks softly.)* What are you doing
            here, Ellen? The mistress is beside herself because she's
            lost her ring . . .

ELLEN: Which ring?

KRISTIN: Her best ring with the blue stone, the one that cost two
            thousand *kronor* – and when she couldn't find you she
            thought . . .

ELLEN: What did she think?

KRISTIN: That you'd run away . . . with the ring.

ELLEN: I never . . . me? And what did you say, Kristin?

KRISTIN: I know you're innocent. When you know somebody well enough you can tell: he or she is innocent and he or she is guilty.

OLD MAN: Are you sure?

KRISTIN: I wouldn't swear on it but I'm sure, anyway.

ELLEN: And now I'm in trouble.

KRISTIN: She's got this fixed idea . . .

ELLEN: But she can tell that I haven't run away.

KRISTIN: It doesn't help.

ELLEN: And if the ring turns up again she'll be angry because I was innocent and because she was wrong. You know, I'll just hand in my notice.

KRISTIN: Don't . . . then she'll be convinced of your guilt and send for the police.

ELLEN: This is going to turn out a nice Christmas!

OLD MAN: *(Getting up.)* Everything will be alright in the end my dears, but first a period of trials and tribulations – after rain comes shine, it never fails – and this is no exception. You're an honest girl, Ellen, but you must learn to be patient.

ELLEN: Aren't I?

OLD MAN: Yes, but there's more to learn. Once again with all my heart: I wish you both a happy Christmas. *(Exits right.)*

ELLEN: I only wish a good conscience was sufficient.

KRISTIN: It goes a long way. Come inside and try to keep calm when the storm breaks.

ELLEN: How can I do that?

KRISTIN: Look at the master. He's also suspected of stealing the ring . . .

ELLEN: Him? Him as well?

KRISTIN: Him as well, yes. But he doesn't fly into a rage, he doesn't get angry . . . just sad. Come now.

ELLEN: Him as well. Then I don't have to feel so bad. Then
                  I'll put up with it.

KRISTIN: Come now. *(They exit right.)*

CHRISTMAS
SPIRIT: *(Enters with a broom.)* Now I shall sweep up for Ellen
                  and Kristin because they're nice girls. But I'll brush
                  the dirt across to Ebba's door because she's not very
                  nice. And then I'll wipe the bench and the ice
                  cupboard . . . and polish the brass – but not for Ebba.
                  That's it! Now let's see what they're up to in there.
                  *(Lights a torch. Thanks to some back-lighting we can see
                  into the vestibule; a white ice box with a white mirror
                  above, a small white chair and underneath it, a child's
                  pair of galoshes. The wife stands in front of the mirror
                  arranging her hair.)* You beautiful young mother, I
                  don't mind you admiring your good looks but you
                  mustn't worship them. It's alright to love your child
                  but you mustn't worship it. I've got a little Christmas
                  card for you somewhere here. *(Searches among a bunch
                  of cards.)* Rhododendron . . . no. Violet . . . no.
                  Snowberry . . . no. Mistletoe . . . no. Thistle . . . yes.
                  I'll give you that one. It has a pretty flower but it's
                  prickly. *(Pushes a Christmas card through the letterbox.)*
                  Let's hear what they're saying in the kitchen. *(Switches
                  the torch off and listens towards the right.)* Ellen's being
                  blamed for stealing a ring. But she hasn't. Ellen doesn't
                  steal. Ebba might. I know everybody in this house. All
                  the gentlefolk and all the servant girls. Ellen is crying. I
                  shall find the ring, I shall search for it from the
                  basement to the attic, in the lift, in the shower rooms,
                  in the vacuum cleaner . . . I know all the corners and
                  crevices in this house, but first I'd better see if they're
                  keeping the ice cupboard tidy. *(Looks into and rummages
                  around in the ice cupboard.)* Yes, that will do.

CHRISTMAS
FAIRY: *(A woman dressed in white with snow stars in her hair.)* What
                  are you up to, silly? Are you eavesdropping . . . that's not
                  very nice.

CHRISTMAS
SPIRIT: What I do is always right . . .
                  I am the custodian of law and order in this house,
                  I punish, comfort, strike and love . . . and clean up.

CHRISTMAS
FAIRY: You have a big house to look after.

CHRISTMAS
SPIRIT: A tower of Babel with all kinds of people
                and languages; six flights of stairs and a basement;
                three apartments on each floor,
                a dozen cradles and seven pianos:
                many people's destinies have been decided here;
                hearts and minds and tempers pull and strain
                like rocks and rafters.
                It hangs together but just about . . .
                and the neighbour – who doesn't know his next-door
                neighbour
                must learn to tolerate and show forbearance . . .
                overlook his neighbour's little whims.
                One plays the piano after ten,
                one rises too early, one's too late to bed.
                It can't be helped, one has to compromise;
                listen to all those little noises
                in the stairwell shell . . .
                The lift is creaking, the pipes are gurgling . . .
                and the central heating simmers like a samovar;
                Listen . . . someone's using the shower,
                there goes the vacuum cleaner.
                A door is shut, a little child is crying,
                here a newly-wed, there a divorcee,
                and over there a widower.
                Jumbled up like their pianinos
                between them producing a waltz,
                a fugue and a sonata.
                In the basement . . . poverty like in the attic,
                in the apartments . . . luxury and show,
                solid assets and hollow lives.
                People make a living, surge forward, scrape along,
                one day someone dies, someone else gets married
                and another sues for a divorce.
                Someone quarrels, moans, makes up . . .
                but when he realises that the struggle is to no avail
                he takes his leave and moves away.

CHRISTMAS
FAIRY: Who lives in there?

CHRISTMAS
SPIRIT: The young wife that everyone is talking about.

CHRISTMAS
FAIRY: I know her then. Yes, I do.
                 Listen to the storm in the kitchen.
                 My dear, is this supposed to be the peaceful season?

CHRISTMAS
SPIRIT: Today is the day before Christmas Eve . . .
                 that's always a busy day in the kitchen.
                 But something else has happened . . .
                 Poor Ellen is blamed unjustly . . .

CHRISTMAS
FAIRY: I know, the cup is full and now it will overflow;
                 the wine of wrath will be pressed from sour grapes.
                 But punishment is not my business;
                 I comfort, help and put things right,
                 I'll let you pull their hair, you've got the right touch
                 . . .
                 Listen! The beautiful little woman who was born
                 to make people happy and to honour the Creator . . .
                 we'll give her a lesson, a short but hard one;
                 she's built her happiness around her little child,
                 and from this her vanity has grown,
                 with vanity comes harshness, cruelty . . .
                 Let's take the little child away from her.
                 Let her feel the loss.
                 Don't worry. She'll have it back tomorrow evening . . .
                 as a Christmas present . . . as a gift, mind you.
                 What are they going to think? They can think what
                 they like!
                 That the child has got lost . . .
                 but you mustn't lie to them.
                 Lies take root like weeds.

CHRISTMAS
SPIRIT: It's too cruel. She won't be able to cope.

CHRISTMAS
FAIRY: She will. I'll help her.
                 She's not without a heart,
                 it's just lacking in goodness, but sorrow will cure her
                 . . .

When the bright sun of happiness begins to burn,
grass and flowers wither . . .
a little cloud gives shade and cools you down;
And clouds give rain, and rain produces greenery.
It's clouding over. – Don't be too hard on her . . . yet
. . .

CHRISTMAS
SPIRIT: *(Sadly)* You don't need to tell me that.
She is so beautiful.

CHRISTMAS
FAIRY: Yes. But we'll make her good as well.
Then happiness will follow . . . of the lasting kind.

CHRISTMAS
SPIRIT: But wait a minute, there's someone in the attic . . .
a poor wretch who is still waiting for his present.

CHRISTMAS
FAIRY: Who is he? Tell me.

CHRISTMAS
SPIRIT: He's a philosopher who is longing for his end.

CHRISTMAS
FAIRY: We have no power over life and death,
but if he's deserved it, he shall have a gift.

CHRISTMAS
SPIRIT: He broods over the riddle of life.

CHRISTMAS
FAIRY: Is that worth brooding over?

CHRISTMAS
SPIRIT: He's an old fool, but he is a kind soul . . .

CHRISTMAS
FAIRY: What's he up to in the attic then?

CHRISTMAS
SPIRIT: He stuffs birds, dries fishes, pins up worms . . .
and has a cupboard full of yellow paper,
where he searches night and day . . .
In that cupboard . . . he searches for the riddle of life!

CHRISTMAS
FAIRY: I know his kind. Yes, he'll get his Christmas present.
Don't worry . . . let's set about it now.

A SHORT BLACK-OUT

SCENE TWO

The vestibule.

*A white ice box to the right, with a white mirror above: on the bottom
shelf a silver brush, on the upper shelf a vase of tulips; underneath the
mirror a hanging basket for gloves. On the ice box lies the Christmas card
with the thistle. To the left, a white chair is placed under a coat-hanger;
under the chair a pair of child's galoshes; on the hanger – a child's white
fur-coat and a white bonnet. No other clothes can be seen. The door at
the back opens to the drawing-room and through a yellow chintz curtain
we can glimpse a sewing table with a beautiful lamp and a bowl with
pretty flowers; behind them the young wife. She wears a white dress with
a square-necked bodice; her dark hair is arranged in a Japanese chignon
which reveals the nape of her neck. She is working on some yellow silk
material which could be a child's garment.*

CHRISTMAS
SPIRIT: *(In the vestibule, picks up the postcard from the ice box.)*
Here's my Christmas card with the thistle!
A little weed among the wheat for you . . .
prickly like you, but it carries a pretty flower . . .
Like you!
You pretty little mother figure. Your hand moves as if
it was picking flowers . . .
and your head – bowed as if in contemplation or
prayer.
Now she smiles because she can hear the child coming
. . .
the little steps on the smooth parquet floor . . .
which was polished yesterday, with beeswax and pine
oil . . .
it smells like conifers in May – when the breams are
jumping in the river and it is time to open up the green
shutters of the summer cottage.
What a beautiful home for beautiful people to live in,

protected against filth and grime . . .
Look at the flowers in the mirror!
The red and yellow turbans of the tulips
are concealing rounded cheeks and budding lips
which meet in chaste embraces,
like waterlilies on the cool reflection of a lake.
Yes, the mirror! There are marks on it – from little
fingers
which have searched for the image behind the glass,
thinking there might be another little girl there.
Look at Rosa on her little mistress' chair
guarding her mistress' coat and boots;
everything that could enhance life
is to be found in there, behind closed doors . . .
but it's not esteemed or valued until too late . . .
I'll switch the light off now. May the dark conceal the
sorrow,
my actions will not stand the scrutiny of daylight.
(Turns the switch. It is dark.)
When the lights come on again, it will be Christmas
Eve. *(Hides behind the curtain to the right.)*

*The Young Wife rings a little bell. Ellen enters with a
lit candle. The Wife is seen chiding her. Ellen cries in
her apron and exits.*

*The Wife comes into the vestibule with the candle
which she puts down on the ice box. There she finds the
Christmas card with the thistle which she reads and
then destroys. After that she looks at herself in the
mirror and tidies her hair.*

*At this point we hear a neighbour playing Beethoven's
Sonata 31, Opus 110 "L'istesso Tempo di Arioso".
The Wife listens. Then she takes the silver brush and
starts brushing the child's clothes. Picks some dirt off
and brushes it again; discovers a loose button, picks up
the doll from the chair and puts it on the ice box; sits
down on the chair, takes a needle and thread from her
bodice and sews the button on. Then she gets up and
takes a black glove from the glove basket. She looks for
the matching one but can't find it; she looks in the
child's galoshes under the chair; she finally puts the
glove in her cleavage and looks confused.*

*The music changes to Beethoven's Funeral March. The
Wife listens and looks frightened. There is a noise
coming from the ice cupboard. It sounds like chunks of
ice collapsing.*

*A child is screaming. The Wife, terrified, wants to get
out but stops still.*

*Someone is banging on a wall; the lift is creaking, the
water pipes are making a noise; people's voices can be
heard off-stage. Kristin enters, pale and with her arms
lifted and her hands clasped. She talks to the Wife but
we can't hear what she says. She rushes out again.*

*The Wife wants to run after her, but can't – falls
down on her knees by the chair and hides her face in
the child's coat which she caresses and hugs.*

    SHORT BLACK-OUT

SCENE THREE

*The Concierge's room. At the back a stained glass pane is lit up from
the outside but now and again it is obscured by the lift.*

*A table laid for Christmas dinner with a white table-cloth and a small
Christmas tree with twisted wax candles; a keg of beer, decorated with fir
twigs stands at the end of the table; buns, a butter dish, a boar's head, a
leg of mutton, half a salmon, a smoked goose etc. A candlestick at the
other end of the table; juniper twigs on the floor; on the wall, a
lithograph depicting the birth of Christ; underneath the print there is a
black board with a lot of keys. A paraffin lamp is burning.*

The Concierge sitting at the table, resting.

OLD MAN: *(Enters with a sheaf of corn for the birds.)* Good day
           again, my dear fellow, are you sitting here all on your
           own . . .

CONCIERGE: The old tree does not grow to maturity, unless it stands
           alone
           in the forest, uncrowded by the young saplings;
           and time has pruned the trees around me.
           (Pause. Motions him to sit down.)

Once I had a whole cottage full . . . it was crowded . . .
I'm not complaining . . . it was warm and comfortable
there with mother and children . . .
but this is not so bad either, maybe better even;
everything is always for the best . . . somehow,
at some time . . .
Now I sit in the shadow of my Christmas tree
and remember the days of yore with gratitude.
I enjoyed those days, after all. There must be many
people
who are regretting bitterly the things they never had,
too late to put it right . . .

OLD MAN: Yes, I've also enjoyed . . . but I'd rather not remember
             . . .

CONCIERGE: Sit down. I was going to say, as a countryman, born
             and bred in a mining district, I feel free . . . I was
             brought up underground, that's why I like it best down
             here in the basement of the Tower of Babel . . . tucked
             away. And I can see daylight through the stained glass
             window which is my sun, obscured now and again by
             the shadow of the lift that passes like a cloudlet.

OLD MAN: Yes, you sit here like the King of the Trolls
             and rule over the elements . . .
             You are the master of fire and heat
             and you portion out the water . . . hot and cold,
             from this dark region you spread light . . .
             you suck up the dust with your vacuum air,
             the dirt that clings to human feet.
             You regulate the lift according to the laws of gravity,
             so people can go up and down on request.

CONCIERGE: In truth, my friend, you exaggerate . . .

OLD MAN: Oh no, you are many more things besides . . .
             I see you have the keys to all the doors in the house,
             and everyone has the key to your heart;
             you know all the fates that are woven here,
             you hear, you see through walls and floors
             and people come to you with their troubles and
             problems
             and confide in you . . .

CONCIERGE: You flatter me too much, Doctor,
but it won't go to my head; I take it with a pinch of
salt,
but you've made me more content with this humble
position,
you've cheered me up,
and transformed my overcrowded hovel into a palace.

OLD MAN: I can hear voices in the vestibule, loud and angry . . .
someone's screaming . . . crying, they'll soon be here;
and you will have to serve as judge
and sort things out, advise and silence when there is a
scene.

CONCIERGE: *(Listens)* I think I know, it's that lovely Ellen . . .
on the third floor . . . who works for the young wife
. . .

OLD MAN: I'll take my corn and go and feed the birds
they're competing with the weather cocks . . .
once again: Happy Christmas to you.

CONCIERGE: The same to you, doctor.

OLD MAN: Just one more thing! What happened to that glove you
found?

CONCIERGE: Oh, that one. I must have dropped it on the stairs
somewhere. No matter, who will miss one glove?

OLD MAN: Don't say that, each half is less than whole without its
other half. *(Exits)*

ELLEN: *(Enters, dressed for outdoors.)* Can I sit down here with
you for a while?

CONCIERGE: By all means, my dear.

ELLEN: I can't stand it any longer; when the electricity went
out they blamed me for it; and then they blamed me
for the ring again; now they've reported it to the police.

CONCIERGE: And this is supposed to be Christmas? You are the
worst family in this house – but let's fix some light
now. *(Takes out some tools.)* My hammer, my tongs . . .
(Takes the keys from the board.) My keys which enable
me to walk through locked doors.

ELLEN: I think the central heating has broken down too.

CONCIERGE: That as well! What are you doing up there? This sort
of thing only happens in your apartment.

ELLEN: It's like a curse. I got frightened, I heard a baby crying
and then there were noises coming from the walls . . . I
think Kristin is leaving too, she can't stand it any
longer.

CONCIERGE: Where is the master then? Is there no master of the
house?

ELLEN: I think he is away hunting . . . we haven't seen him for
two whole days . . . he couldn't stand it either. But it's
like the old doctor says: they're too well off. Nothing to
do, no appetite, no sleep. Their only problem is how to
get rid of the money.

CONCIERGE: But they don't want to pay people who work for them.
Oh no!

ELLEN: Haven't you had any Christmas box either?

CONCIERGE: No. She got upset because I asked her not to stand up
in the lift . . . I said it in rather a sharp tone, I
suppose, because I was in a hurry.

ELLEN: Shhh, I can hear Kristin on the stairs. She puts up
with more than me, but even she's got her limits.

CONCIERGE: Isn't it funny . . . to some people money is not a
blessing . . . I suppose that's a comfort to us in a way.
Where did they get their money from?

ELLEN: They must have inherited it . . . shhh, here she is.
Something else must have taken place in that ghost
apartment.

CONCIERGE: Why not call it the ghost house? So many strange
things take place here . . . it's as if all these machines
brought something else with them . . . Ebba says she's
seen the Christmas Spirit sitting on the roof of the lift
holding on to the wires.

*The Christmas Spirit swops the keys around on the
board.*

ELLEN: I could actually believe in gremlins because sometimes
you don't find things where you put them, sometimes a

lock gets jammed, and sometimes you get hot water
coming out of the cold tap.

CONCIERGE: *(Listens)* Anyone there? I thought I heard someone
rattling with the keys . . . *(The Christmas Spirit hides.
Concierge searches among the keys.)* I think the devil
must have mixed these keys up. We've got 25 on 13
and 17 on 81. And the merchant's card has ended up in
the magistrate's pigeon-hole. And there's always people
talking on the stairs. They quarrel and cry but when I
turn up they're gone.

ELLEN: But I can hear Kristin now . . . you can always tell
when it's her.

CONCIERGE: *(Pretending to open a door to the left.)* There's not a
living soul here . . .

ELLEN: You frighten me. Sometimes it's the children's voices
. . . sometimes it's the pigeons on the roof . . .
sometimes I think it must be the old professor upstairs
making fun of us . . . Who is he anyway?

CONCIERGE: He is a strange chap. But he is a kind fellow.

ELLEN: Didn't you find a glove on the stairs?

CONCIERGE: Yes, the professor found one and I was going to look
after it but I lost it, I'm afraid.

ELLEN: You've lost it, and there was such a commotion upstairs
about that glove! Just as much as about the ring.

The telephone rings.

CONCIERGE: *(On the telephone.)* Yes, she's sitting right here beside
me. No, that's impossible. She doesn't steal any rings.
We know our Ellen. She's not a thief. It's unfair. But
I'll tell her. *(Puts the receiver down.)*

ELLEN: I understand. It was the police, wasn't it?

CONCIERGE: Yes, my dear. They've summoned you to the station.

ELLEN: I'd rather drown myself.

CONCIERGE: But go to the police station first.

ELLEN: Never, they'll never let me go.

CONCIERGE: Look at me, Ellen! And don't expect the worst. Go in peace.

ELLEN: *(Looks at him and is finally persuaded by him.)* Alright, I'll go then . . . I looked into your eyes and I listened to you . . . now I feel safe. *(The Concierge accompanies her out.)* And this hand's given me strength. It guides me, it supports me. I'm going. *(Exits)*

      Pause.

AN OLD
LADY: *(Enters with the black glove and a little brown child's boot.)* Look what I found in the lift. Do you happen to know who they belong to? You did get your Christmas money, didn't you?

CONCIERGE: Yes, thank you. That's the missing glove. *(Puts it on the table beside the boot.)*

AN OLD
LADY: You've got your Christmas table laid, I see . . . and a tree and lots of food . . . a smoked pig's head! I say!

CONCIERGE: A rich lady like you surely doesn't begrudge a poor man . . .?

AN OLD
LADY: You're not as poor as you look. And I'm not as rich as I look. Look after this glove now so it doesn't get lost again. It's bible-black but it conceals a white hand and maybe something else as well. *(Exits)*

CONCIERGE: *(Baffled)* But the little boot . . . the heel is worn at the side, naughty little thing . . . *(The Christmas Spirit has taken the glove and hides it.)* It belongs to a little child, impossible to say whether a boy or a girl because there is no difference between right and left at that age – no difference between good and evil – they're all children of God. But later on! Oh dear. *(He wants to put the glove away.)* But where is the glove? I put it down on the table here. *(Searches)* It's gone. *(Searches)*

KRISTIN: *(Stands in the room, in despair.)* Just think, think, think . . .

CONCIERGE: What is it? Who is it? Kristin!

KRISTIN: Imagine . . . God help us! The little girl is gone!

CONCIERGE: Gone? What do you mean?

KRISTIN: She's lost. Someone has abducted her . . .

CONCIERGE: Impossible! I would have noticed . . . I would have heard. I'm here to look after the house and the people who live in it.

KRISTIN: Don't you know anything about it? Then I'll go to the police station. Be kind to the young mother when she comes, won't you? She sat upstairs without light and heating. It's too cruel, even to someone like her. *(Exits)*

CONCIERGE: What's all this? There's something unnatural about this, that's for sure. And that means there is still hope. *(He puts the boot on the table.)* Who is coming? The poor little mother herself. *(He hides to the right.)*

YOUNG WIFE: *(Enters from left dressed just like in the first act.)*
Where have I got to?
And where am I?
Where did I come from?
Who am I?
It must be a poor person living here . . . but he's got so many keys!
Is it a hotel?
No, a prison, an underground prison . . .
There shines the moon, it looks like a heart
and the clouds march past in black . . .
There's a forest, a forest of conifers,
a Christmas forest full of gifts and lights . . .
Inside the prison? No, this is some other place.
Anyone at home?

CONCIERGE: *(Visible to the right but only to the audience. Aside.)*
She is beside herself with grief, she has lost her memory
. . .
A mercy, a mercy for someone who's suffering.

YOUNG WIFE: But wait! I remember, but the memory is behind . . .
and I went ahead to look for something.
What was I looking for?
A glove that I'd lost. It was black . . .
Now it's black again!
But I can see something blue in the dark,

like the sky in the spring . . . appearing between white
clouds,
a mountain lake between steep shores,
that's how blue my sapphire was . . . that I lost . . .
the one they've stolen . . .
I've lost a lot of things these last few days . . .
I was cold and I was sitting in the dark . . .

It's warm but stuffy here;
the weight of the high tower at the top,
the heavy burden of human destinies,
I can feel them pressing me down, towards the earth
. . .
pressing my heart in its weak rib-cage . . .
I wanted to speak but I couldn't find the words . . .
I wanted to cry as if I was grieving!
(Catches sight of the boot.)
What's this? A little boot?
A little stocking and a foot? In you go!
What was that? Here is a candle
that's sprouted branches, it's grown
from the root of the candlestick and soon
it will burst into flower,
three blue-white flowers with a bit of red inside . . .
I didn't know that candles could grow and sprout
twigs.
Which part of the world have I got to?
An anchor buoy is floating in a forest here,
a wild boar's head is sticking up from the sea,
and the fish are walking on dry land.
(Sees the print of the birth of Christ.)
What's this? – A crib in a stable?
(Starts to wake up.)
And the shepherd's brown cows look with their big
eyes,
at the little child . . . who . . . is asleep in the crib.
(Wakes up and screams.)
Oh Jesus Christ, save me!
I'm dying. I'm dying. – A child is born this night, a
child has died. There is the concierge . . . he is angry
with me because I didn't give him a Christmas box.
Don't be angry with me! Don't take revenge. I'll give
you all my rings . . .

CONCIERGE: *(Steps forward.)* I'm not angry, I'm not going to take any revenge; your child will come back, a child can't just get lost in a city like this . . . come with me now, I'll give you some heating and lighting in the meantime . . .

YOUNG WIFE: Say that again . . . a child can't get lost in a city . . . I don't believe you, of course – but say it anyway! Say it many times . . .

CONCIERGE: Come with me, but while I repair the machinery you must go upstairs and get warm. Go to your old friend on the third floor. He can talk, I can't . . . and he'll comfort you . . .

YOUNG WIFE: Do you mean the gentleman? I suppose he's angry with me too?

CONCIERGE: No one here is angry with you. Come on now.

YOUNG WIFE: You're so kind to me; you're not going to take revenge?

CONCIERGE: Oh dear, dear. What a wicked person you are, madam!

YOUNG WIFE: But my child! My child! My child!

CONCIERGE: Come on now!

CURTAIN

SCENE FOUR

The garret.

At the back, light green curtains are drawn across two windows: On a column between the two windows there is a manuscript cupboard with a beautiful lamp on top: To the left, an oak table full of manuscripts: To the right an easy chair.

CHRISTMAS
SPIRIT: *(Enters)* It's Christmas Eve, but up here in the old philosopher's place there is no sign of the joyous season.
(Draws the curtains back.)
But . . . he's put his Christmas tree on the balcony.
The sheaf of corn with its thousand beaks,
one grain each to feed the birds of heaven;

the sparrows and the pigeons;
they're still asleep on the tin roofs
with their heads under their wings . . .
soon the morning breeze will shake the vanes
on the chimney-stacks above the stoves,
where fires are crackling happily
while heating up the coffee pots;
then I'll run along the roof tops
and enjoy the smells . . .
as the morning sun casts its rays
on the telephone wires . . .
Then the wires and the vanes will sing
and the pigeons will cuddle up in their fillets,
in the meantime, the children leave their beds . . .

What's he got here?
He's collected all his knowledge
on sheets of yellow paper, thousands and thousands of
them.
Straw in a hot-house
threshed husks; no, finely ground fodder
where you have to search for the grains . . .
and he's collected the kernels in this barn
of carved oak, there lies the harvest . . .
(Opens the cupboard.)
This is the table of contents, the key to his wisdom,
the riddle of creation which he believes he's solved.
You old fool you've organised it all so well . . .
Now I shall mess it up, this rubbish that
you've collected in the hills;
I'll bring chaos again
so that you have to start from the beginning.
(Jumbles up the manuscripts.)
Here are the wise man's specs.
He's got short-sighted with the years . . .
I shall give you a present
which will make you far-sighted and foresighted.
*(Exchanges the glasses for another pair which he takes out
of his pocket.)*
I shall give you new eyes
so you can see what's invisible
to normal mortals!
Where you used to see laws

you'll now meet the law-maker,
and later on the Judge;
where you used to see mischief
caused by nature and blind fate,
you will find creatures of
the same kind as yourself!

The old man is waking up . . .
maybe he's kept vigil
because night is like day
for those who study in the dark!
Here he comes, I'll stay
and say hello and get to know him. *(Withdraws through the right curtain.)*

OLD MAN: *(Enters from left, dressed in black with a white cravat, black silk cap, long white hair and a similar beard.)*
Welcome life! Good morning, labour!
For sixty years I've organised the universe . . .
now the dawn is breaking on the day
when I shall solve the riddle . . .
Everything lies there like stratifications of the earth,
deposited gradually from fire and water . . .
from stones and herbs and animals,
organic matter, forces, measures and numbers;
I've collected the building blocks
for the heavenly staircase in the Tower of Babel,
I shall climb from the vale of tears
and seize the mosque with its blue cupola
which rests on the four points of the compass.

For sixty years I've collected, counted;
and once, at half-time I found the riddle.
One night . . . I wrote it down on a piece of paper
but it got buried and then it vanished . . .
It's there somewhere but while I've been searching
the pile has grown into a haystack,
and my own child has grown into a giant . . .
I'm beaten back as I get closer,
it's like digging for a treasure,
with the spade falling out of my mind,
my head gets tired, my body's growing old.
And I often ended up paralysed
when I wanted to overview it all . . .

Now I feel the hour has come,
because in a dream I had last night I saw . . .
I saw the paper I'd been looking for;
it was a blue-white vellum with a water mark
of English origin . . .
(Takes his cuff links off.)
Now or never! It's between you and me,
you pile of papers, yield your secret now;
Hear me, spirits, I'm your master,
I alone rule here.
(Puts on his glasses and searches among the papers.)
What's this? What's this?
I can't find my old order,
the alphabet and numbers have changed places,
a,b,c,d,h,r, I'm damned . . .
and the numbers: 1, 7, 4, 10, 26, someone's been here!
Alpha, beta, pi, and the cipher I invented . . .
I've quite forgotten now . . . it's gone from my mind
. . .
(Goes on searching.)
Here's a clue but there is an ink stain on the main
figure . . .
I'll blot it out.
(Picks up a knife.)
Now I've made a hole in the paper! Oh well, I'll go on
searching;
I'll look through every scrap of paper until I find it.
(Looks at sheet after sheet.)
The neighbour starts playing again! Play on. I don't
mind. I've got the whole day ahead of me. And the
night as well. I don't eat anything, I don't need any
sleep. *(For a few minutes while the Old Man is moving
various papers around someone is playing Beethoven's
Sonata 29, Opus 106, Adagio Sostenuto.)* I'm getting
tired quickly today. I'll take a rest. *(Collapses onto the
easy chair. The music continues.)* My eyesight has
become so strange. Things next to me seem so far away
and things at a distance seem to come closer. And my
head is empty. *(He closes his eyes. The music continues.
He wakes up and attacks the pile of papers again, but
soon gets tired and returns to his chair; attacks again but
is pushed back. Now he falls asleep in the chair and looks
lifeless. The Christmas Spirit pushes another chair in from*

*the right and sits down nonchalantly in front of the Old
Man. The music stops. The Old Man wakes up.)* Who's
there? Are you real . . .

CHRISTMAS
SPIRIT: To be is to be perceived,
             you have perceived me:
             therefore I exist.

OLD MAN: *(Gets up.)* But I want to feel you, I want to touch you.
             Otherwise you don't exist for me.

CHRISTMAS
SPIRIT: You cannot touch the rainbow, but it's real all the
             same.
             So is the mirage when you're in the desert or at sea . . .
             I'm a mirage, don't come too close,
             because then you won't see me
             even though I do exist.

OLD MAN: There's logic in what you say . . .

CHRISTMAS
SPIRIT: Well, then you must believe what you see . . .
             (The Old Man grumbles.)
             You grumble because I don't fit into your system . . .
             and your system is your master,
             and you its servant . . .

OLD MAN: I rule supreme in my system.

CHRISTMAS
SPIRIT: Then tell me, in a few words
             what is the essence of all those facts
             that you've collected there, or have you just collected
             leaves,
             rain drops, sand granules, which resemble each other
             but are not the same.

OLD MAN: My philosophy derived from all those
             millions of incidents that occur . . .

CHRISTMAS
SPIRIT: Let's hear. I'm eager to learn.

OLD MAN: You thief, you stole my thought from me;
             a minute ago it was all so clear . . .

CHRISTMAS
SPIRIT: And now? It was muddied like crystal clear ice
            when it melts in the heat; it turned into slush,
            and then water that evaporated in a flash.
            It evaporated. I'll solidify it again
            and explain your system . . . which you've forgotten.
            (Pause)
            In the unity of the whole you'll see the meaning of life.

OLD MAN: Exactly. You're a clever fellow
            who's discovered what I've been looking for these last
            thirty years.
            The unity of matter. That's the word.

CHRISTMAS
SPIRIT: That was the system. Now back to reality.
            Ponder the duality of nature and let's see
            if that's not a more reliable theory.
            (Pause)
            The wet element, water, is one substance
            but it's beyond dispute that it's made up of two:
            hydrogen and oxygen;
            the magnetic powers are divided into north and south;
            the electrical into plus and minus;
            the flower seeds contain both male and female
            and highest in the chain, right at the top
            you'll find duality as well, because it
            wasn't good for man to be alone;
            that's why man and woman were created;
            Quod est demonstrandum.

OLD MAN: You little devil. You have taken it apart . . .

CHRISTMAS
SPIRIT: Your toy, silly; your chain has broken
            and lies there now in scattered links,
            your cable that you twisted has been straightened out
            and become ropes, ready for the scrap merchant.

OLD MAN: Ha! Sixty years to blow a bubble
            which bursts in the first draught.
            Now there's no point in going on.

CHRISTMAS
SPIRIT: If the bubble bursts you can blow new ones,
            they're made of water and of frothy soap,

which has been whisked up to make it bigger
but it's so small, almost nothing . . .

OLD MAN: And sixty years . . .
(Angry, rises and throws the papers to the left.)
Out! Damned fantasy!
A rotten fruit of twenty thousand days' of labour.
Out! Out! You dry leaves which have worn my tree
down.
Lamplighters, Bengalian fires put me on the wrong
path,
misled me to the bog where I sank to my neck in mud,
enticed me into deserts where prickly bushes tore my
hands . . .
(Empties the cupboard of papers but leaves one box alone.)
These false pilots made me go aground,
these guides pointed to the road to hell;
bankrupt, destitute, I now give up the claim
and sit here empty-handed on the burnt site . . .
(Sinks into the chair.)
a snail that got its shell crushed,
a spider whose web was torn,
a bird that strayed too far into the ocean,
could not turn back and reach the shore . . .
He flaps his wings above a moving abyss . . .
until he falls down exhausted – and dies.
(Pause)

CHRISTMAS
SPIRIT: Tell me, do you want to start from the beginning
again?
Become young again?

OLD MAN: Become young? No thank you. Strong enough to suffer,
strong enough to weave false dreams? No thank you.

CHRISTMAS
SPIRIT: Do you want riches?

OLD MAN: What for? I don't wish for anything else . . . except to
die.

CHRISTMAS
SPIRIT: I see. But you have to reconcile yourself with life first.

OLD MAN: Reconcile? Be tied again to the pillory?
              No, out of the question; then there will be no departure . . .
              "One more handshake and one for the road. Stay a
              little longer." Then you're stuck.
              No, up on the seat and whip the jade,
              tear yourself away and no looking back.

CHRISTMAS
SPIRIT: You broke away once from throbbing life
              from home and hearth and wife and children,
              to chase the empty shells of fame and glory.

OLD MAN: Half true. I left in time,
              to avoid seeing the others leave . . . who'd already
              packed.
              When life betrayed me, when the ship was about to
              sink,
              I made a lifebuoy which I inflated,
              so far you're right;
              it kept me afloat for a while, quite a while in fact;
              then it burst and I sank, is that my fault?

CHRISTMAS
SPIRIT: *(Has taken the box out of the cupboard.)*
              Here are some shipwrecked goods washed ashore . . .

OLD MAN: *(Powerless)* Leave my box alone. Don't wake up the
              dead.

CHRISTMAS
SPIRIT: Like the Sadducees you don't believe in the
              resurrection;
              so why do you fear the dead?

OLD MAN: Leave my box alone. You raise up spirits . . .

CHRISTMAS
SPIRIT: Yes. In order to show you that life is spirit
              imprisoned in a body, in matter.
              Watch out, because I shall raise them now,
              I'm about to conjure.
              (Opens the box.)

OLD MAN: Oh! The scent! Is it clover?
              In rosy May when the apple trees have burst into
              blossom
              and the lilacs rock their spires to the westerly wind

and freshly dug gardens . . . which recently lay white
with snow . . . stretch their black cloth
over covered seeds which are buried for rebirth.
(Sinding's 'Frühlingsrauschen' is played)
I can see a little country cottage, white with green
shutters,
a window opens and the curtain flutters,
it's made of burgundy coloured chintz; right at the
back of the mirror, in a gilt frame – empire style –
and in the oval glass I can see . . .
like a mirage . . . the most beautiful thing in life . . .
a young mother dressing her child,
and combing its soft curls, wiping the sleep
out of its blue eyes which open
and smile towards the sun and mother,
full of desire for living . . .
The little foot stamps the carpet
impatiently like a frisky colt, eager to run free . . .
Music! Which notes from my youth,
half forgotten are now revived again?
The rivulet which meanders past the alderberry trees
a boat, midsummer wreaths, wild strawberry baskets,
and freshly caught pike wriggling in the boat . . .
(Christmas Spirit picks up a small bridal crown and veil.)
What do I see? What's that?
A little crown of myrtle, for a little queen,
and a veil of tulle . . .
morning mist round a fairy ring at sunrise.
Now I can't see any more, my eye is veiled . . .
Oh Lord, all this was real once
but is no more and will never come back.
(Cries and breaks down.)

CHRISTMAS
SPIRIT :   All this was yours and you threw it away,
fresh flowers in exchange for dry leaves,
warm life for cold reason,
you poor man . . . but what is this?
(Shows him a black ladies' glove.)

OLD MAN :   A little glove! May I see? I don't remember . . .
how did it get here? Wait, now I recall . . .
yesterday morning I found it on the stairs . . .

CHRISTMAS
SPIRIT: I'll give it to you as a Christmas present . . .
It's full of secrets and the tiny fingers
have meddled in people's destinies, sown evil,
but she extends her hand of friendship to you now;
If you take it, as I expect you will,
you'll spread some happiness and solve a riddle
which is of greater value than the ancient riddle
that's bothered you.
(Locks the box in the cupboard.)

OLD MAN: If I can still make someone happy,
and someone looks at me with gratitude,
If I can touch a person to the heart,
then my despair can still be cured.

CHRISTMAS
SPIRIT: You've burnt your dying old forest . . .
that was the bravest, wisest thing you've done,
now sow on the burnt site, ashes are good for growth,
and there is still time for a few more harvests. *(Pause)*
But if you can't enjoy them yourself,
then give because it is more blessed to give than to
take, and sacrifices please . . .
Now I'll return to my dark shed
and wish you a very merry Christmas.
(Disappears)

OLD MAN: *(Alone, looking at the glove.)*
A little hand held out in the dark . . .
a gauntlet thrown, not for battle but for peace!
A child's hand, soft and cuddly . . .
What secrets do you hide,
perhaps you're just a dummy,
who turns up for Christmas with a gift . . .
(There is a knock on the door.)
Come in, stranger, there's a present
for the first one who enters. – Come in!

ELLEN: *(Enters)* Excuse me, sir . . . Doctor . . . for barging in
like this,
but you're known as a philanthropist . . .
I'm lost, deserted, in despair.

OLD MAN: *(Gets up.)* God bless you, my child, sit down,
            what happened, is it about the ring?

ELLEN: I've been to the station, and I'm still under suspicion,
            they're looking for me, I wanted to drown myself,
            but I couldn't; let me stay here;
            say something, say that I'm innocent.

OLD MAN: Calm down, and let me think . . .
            what was it now . . . oh yes, here's a present
            from a stranger.

ELLEN: What, an old glove!

OLD MAN: Yes, I don't understand, but someone has lost it
            and someone else has found it, lost it again and refound
            it . . .

ELLEN: I think it belongs to my mistress. Let's see what size it
            is.
            (Turns the glove, the ring falls out.)
            My God! Here's the ring.
            Then I'm saved. You didn't know?

OLD MAN: I didn't know. Dry your tears.

ELLEN: You're so kind. I already knew that you were good to
            animals and flowers.

OLD MAN: Shhh. It's not worth mentioning . . .

ELLEN: Is rescuing a human being not worth mentioning?

OLD MAN: I was just the instrument.

ELLEN: You must be happy now; I wish I were in your place,
            it must be nice to make someone else so happy . . .

OLD MAN: Go and put things back in order
            and rejoice with the others . . .

ELLEN: I can't. The little child is gone,
            how can we enjoy ourselves in a house of sorrow?

OLD MAN: The little child? Yes, I heard the story . . .
            but believe me Ellen, people are playing games here.
            I don't know any more. But if you look at it another
            way . . .

I hope, I think . . . that before the day is over,
everyone will struggle through and get the better of it.
(Leans back in his chair and falls asleep.)

CURTAIN

SCENE FIVE

The nursery. At the back a beautiful curtain which serves as a room divider; a small table in front; on the table two lit candles in silver candlesticks flanking a portrait of a child with flowers; a mirror is placed behind the candles, so the flames are reflected in the mirror. To the left a child's white cot with a blue canopy. To the right a little child's table in white, with a small chair. Rosa, the doll, sits on the chair: presents and a small Christmas tree are placed on the table. A white rocking horse beside the bed.

YOUNG WIFE: *(Enters, dressed in a black coat. She wears a black veil which she tears into pieces and then hangs on various objects around the room: The Christmas tree, the doll, the rocking horse etc.)*
We're in mourning. But something else fills the void;
a chill that cools,
a darkness that conceals;
like the bed-cover you want to pull over you
when you have a sleepless night and try to
flee from images of terror.
Rosa, do you miss your little mistress?
Your cheeks are so pale and your hands so cold;
is the tree going to play its funeral hymn for you?
(She winds up a musical box and puts it under the tree.)
And the horse Blanka with its mourning ribbon around
its arm . . .
I remember last year . . . we went away
to mother and father in the country,
and you stood here alone in the cold room
but Mary thought of you, yes,
"now poor Blanka stands there freezing
and maybe she is afraid of the dark in that gloomy
room."
When she got back you'd caught a cold,
you had a sore throat and she looked after you,

and tied her best stocking around your neck,
she kissed your white nose,
she combed your mane and tied a gold ribbon
on your forehead. You were well looked after,
but now, now we're all suffering, all of us.
The little bed stands empty like a life-raft
when the ship has sunk; it rocks blind drunk.
Who shall I make the bed for,
my little one who's dead?
I remember the last evening
when after supper you got some crumbs
in your bed and I had to remake it,
you thought it was sand that had been strewn
by the sandman like I used to tell you.
I would mix your prayers with fairy tales
and songs to accompany you on your pleasant trip
to the green forests and blue lakes of dreams.
And your eyelids closed like daisies
on the rosy cheeks under your fairy grass hair.
Not here any more! A little hollow in the soft mattress
is the only thing that reminds me of your delicate body.
Under the blue canopied sky
which is now black and overcast . . .
Where is my child? Where are you, answer me.
Have you gone to the stars to play with other children,
not yet born, maybe dead and reborn?
Have you gone to seek the fairy tales
and meet Tom Thumb, Blue Bird
The Red Riding Hood and little Soliman,
when you got tired of us and our squabbles?
I wish I could come with you! I never felt at home
here.
It held out promises that it didn't live up to . . .
It resembled, but was not . . .
a work of art perhaps, but badly flawed,
too much body and too little soul,
and how tragic that one could not be . . .
could not become what one most wanted to be.
(Pause)
But it's dark. They have cut off the light . . .
(Turns a light switch in vain.)
And it's cold, they begrudge me heating.
(Stretches out her hand as if looking for a tap.)

And no water. My flowers are thirsty.
(She rings a little bell.)
But no one comes. Everyone has gone away.
Was I so bad? No one knows
what everyone knows . . . think they know.
Everyone was fawning on me and no one dared
tell me how I ought to be.
Yes, the mirror did, but it wasn't a good friend.
Its smooth glass only uttered politenesses.
(Pause)
What's this? My lost glove.
And here, inside the finger is my ring!
Then she wasn't guilty after all, poor Ellen.
Now she'll take revenge, she'll punish me,
and the end will be worse than the beginning.
To prison? I don't want that . . . I'll hide the ring.
(Pause)
No! Yes! What was that? Someone stroked my cheek.
Is someone there? I heard someone whispering.
A child breathing in her sleep.
And now . . . it's the weathercock on the neighbour's
roof.
Shhh, he's singing on top of the chimney . . .
What does he say: "My Mary, Mary, Mary!"
And then: "Ellen, Ellen". Poor Ellen!
A bell is ringing. The ambulance!
What's happened here? What have I done?
No, fair is fair, when I've done something wrong
I must go and take my punishment.

Ellen enters. The Young Wife kneels in front of her.

ELLEN: Get up for God's sake. You make me unhappy, poor
            dear lady, get up, I can't look at you like that. It isn't
            worth talking about . . . a mistake, that's all, everything
            is so complicated, living isn't easy; it's almost
            impossible, someone said once. There, there.

YOUNG WIFE: Ellen, forgive me!

ELLEN: I already have, I have, dear kind, madam. Get up and
            I'll tell you something . . .

YOUNG WIFE: *(Gets up.)* Is it about . . .?

ELLEN: No, it's not. It's about someone else. The old man in the attic . . . has died . . . contented and reconciled with this thing he was talking about . . . But when we looked through his papers we found his proper name . . . and . . .

YOUNG WIFE: Don't tell me, I know. He was my long-lost father!

ELLEN: Yes.

YOUNG WIFE: And he died without seeing me again. I want to see him. This strange house, where human destinies are piled on top of each other like so many floors and put in a row side by side. Where is my husband? Have you heard from him?

ELLEN: He'll be back for supper. But not before.

YOUNG WIFE: For the Christmas dinner? When it's dark, cold and draughty; in a house full of sorrow and death . . . my poor husband. I'll go and see my father. How did he die, Ellen?

ELLEN: He burnt his papers and said it was all rubbish . . . and it was he who found the ring. And after he'd made me ever so happy he said: Now I can die contented, now that God's granted me the grace to make *one* person happy.

YOUNG WIFE: He was right. I didn't love him. But I want to close his eyes and do him the last favour . . . it's my duty. Come with me, Ellen. *(They leave.)*

> *Pause. Kristin and the Concierge walk across the stage slowly with tools in their hands.*

CONCIERGE: It will be alright. It will be alright.

KRISTIN: *(Pointing at the little bed.)* Shhh. Shhh . . . *(They tiptoe out again.)*

> *The Christmas Spirit to the right and the Christmas Fairy to the left.*

CHRISTMAS
FAIRY: Now our work is almost done . . .
I've seen her kneeling, heard her say
two little words, 'forgive me'; that makes up for everything.
Now it's said, now it's done . . .
Stop grieving. May the joyous feast begin!

CHRISTMAS
SPIRIT: *(Tiptoes around and takes the black bits of veil away from
             the various objects.)*
             I blow the dust away, I sweep and tidy
             I polish the brass which was made dull by foul
             breathing,
             I water the flowers when the maid forgets,
             so they won't be thirsty.
             (He waters the flowers by the mirror.)
             I arrange the curtains in neat folds,
             smooth the carpet; I can also mess things up,
             but not here and not today.
             You little mother, you lovely young wife,
             now that you've suffered, don't forget the lesson!
             From tears of regret and pain
             your eyes become so mild and beautiful, so clear.
             But when you cry with anger you look ugly.
             Now, my angel, it is time to say: Season's greetings!

CHRISTMAS
FAIRY: She comes from a labour of love,
             she has closed her father's eyes . . .
             who only got his child back after death . . .
             *(The Christmas Spirit looks in the bed, rocks it gently,
             lifts his finger as if saying: She is asleep.)*
             Now she'll get hers back, alive . . .
             It's time to turn the knobs, taps and switches on again.

CHRISTMAS
SPIRIT: I'll go and prepare everything for the happy end.

             *They leave in different directions. Pause. Music:
             Sinding's "Frühlingsrauschen".*

YOUNG WIFE: *(Enters as before in a black coat.)*
             Oh, lovely heating. Is it back on again?
             Is it a southerly wind, has the wintry sun risen
             from the equator, is it summer?
             *(Full illumination on the stage. Lets her black coat drop
             onto the floor.)*
             Oh God! One word and there was light!
             Have you opened your sky again?
             Then I'll see a little face
             smiling between white clouds,
             little hands stretching out, a little mouth . . .

But shhh!

(She listens as if she heard a noise coming from the bed: looks around.)

And here! What's happened, is the period of mourning over?

(Walks across to the bed, notices the child, which can't be seen by the audience.)

Yes, the Lord took and the Lord gave back again,

I haven't deserved it yet . . .

(Kneeling in front of the bed.)

But when a mother is allowed to hold her child in her arms,

then happiness has no words, oh happy tears!

> *The Christmas Spirit is visible to the right: he takes his cap off and blows kisses to the mother and child.*

CURTAIN

FURTHER PLAYS AVAILABLE FROM ABSOLUTE CLASSICS

PAINS OF YOUTH
Ferdinand Bruckner
Translated by Daphne Moore

'Discovery of the Year'
GUARDIAN

£4.95

A FAMILY AFFAIR
Alexander Ostrovsky
Adapted by Nick Dear

'a stinging and scurrilously funny version by Nick Dear'
OBSERVER

£4.95

THUNDER IN THE AIR
August Strindberg
Translated by Eivor Martinus

'a sulphurous, atmospheric work full of summer lightning'
GUARDIAN

£4.95

TURCARET
Alain-René Lesage
Translated/adapted by John Norman

'One of the best of French comedies'
SUNDAY TELEGRAPH

£4.95

THE POWER OF DARKNESS
Leo Tolstoy
Translated/adapted by Anthony Clark

'THE POWER OF DARKNESS rends the air with greatness'
SPECTATOR

£4.95

ANATOL
Arthur Schnitzler
Translated by Michael Robinson

'Schnitzler's most amusing and original play'
DAILY TELEGRAPH

£4.95

THERESE RAQUIN
Emile Zola
Translated by Pip Broughton

'A gripping yarn'
GUARDIAN

£4.95

FALSE ADMISSIONS, SUCCESSFUL STRATEGIES, LA DISPUTE
Marivaux
Translated by Timberlake Wertenbaker

'the most successful English translator of Marivaux in the present age, if not ever'
OBSERVER

£5.95

FUENTE OVEJUNA, LOST IN A MIRROR
Lope de Vega
Adapted by Adrian Mitchell

'It is hard to imagine a more gripping tale than the one which emerges in Adrian Mitchell's translation'
TIME OUT

£5.95

THE LIAR, THE ILLUSION
Pierre Corneille
Translated/adapted by Ranjit Bolt

Two contrasting plays from one of France's major classic playwrights in an elegant new translation.

£.5.95

MAN, BEAST AND VIRTUE
Luigi Pirandello
A new version by Charles Wood

'There's no doubting the brilliance of this 1919 farce'
INDEPENDENT

£4.95

THE GREAT HIGHWAY
August Strindberg
Translated by Eivor Martinus

Published April 1990

£4.95

BERENICE
Racine
LE MISANTHROPE, THE SCHOOL FOR WIVES
Molière
Adapted by Neil Bartlett

Published May 1990

£5.95

SARA
Translated by Ernest Bell
MINNA VON BARNHELM
Translated by Anthony Meech
Gotthold Lessing

Published April 1990

£5.95

NANA
Adapted by Olwen Wymark
GERMINAL
Adapted by William Gaminara
From the novels of Emile Zola

Published June 1990

£5.95